T3-BPX-810

PATTERNS
OF
RESIDENTIAL SEGREGATION

Patterns
of
Residential Segregation

by

LINTON C. FREEMAN
University of Hawaii

and

MORRIS H. SUNSHINE
Kent State University

SCHENKMAN PUBLISHING COMPANY
ONE STORY STREET
CAMBRIDGE, MASS. 02138

Copright © 1970
SCHENKMAN PUBLISHING COMPANY
One Story Street
Cambridge, Massachusetts 02138

Printed in the United States of America
Library of Congress Catalog Number
74-76270

SBN 8707-3032-0

Table of Contents

Preface vii
1. Introduction 1
    1.1 The Need for Theory
    1.2 Strategies for Building Theory
    1.3 A Theory of Ethnic Residence
2. The Neighborhood Housing Market Process 7
    2.1 Time
    2.2 A Neighborhood Housing Market
    2.3 Initiating the Market Process: Neighborhood
           Out-migration
    2.4 Setting the Initial Selling Price
    2.5 The Buyer
    2.6 The Transaction
    2.7 Readjusting the Selling Price
3. Simulation of the Neighborhood Housing Market 18
    3.1 The Normal Housing Market
    3.2 The Ghost Town
    3.3 The Boom Town
4. The Nature of Segregation 30
    4.1 Segregation: Intuitive Background
    4.2 Segregation: A Measure
5. The Market with Ethnic Constraints 40
    5.1 Prejudice
    5.2 The Economy and the Lender

        5.3   The Role of the Broker
        5.4   Refusal to Sell
        5.5   Hostile Reactions
        5.6   The Ghetto Phenomenon
6.   Simulation of the Market with Ethnic Constraints 56
        6.1   An Ideal: the Color-Blind Neighborhood
        6.2   The Social Class Ghetto: Economically Based
              Segregation
        6.3   The Classical Case: Invasion and Succession
        6.4   The Reservation: A South African Neighborhood
              Type
        6.5   The Ethnically Mixed Neighborhood: A Possible
              Type
7.   In Conclusion: Some Comments on the Theory 75
        7.1   Findings and Implications for Policy
        7.2   Some Needed Revisions
Glossary of Symbols 83
Bibliography 85
Flow Chart of the Computer Program 88
Computer Output.. 89

Preface

This is a report of a study of ethnic residential segregation. It is not an empirical investigation, but an attempt at organizing the findings of previous research through computer simulation. Thus, we have tried to construct a preliminary theory of residential segregation.

In the conduct of our study and in the preparation of this report we have had two main aims: (1) to take at least a small step in the solution of a major social problem, and (2) to present a detailed example of an exercise in computer simulation.

With respect to the first aim, it is unnecessary to state that racial discrimination—particularly with respect to the Negro—is one of the most important issues in America today. This issue stems from the flagrant contradiction between the fundamental principles of American democracy and the actual social and political status of Negroes.

Moreover, residential segregation is central in the maintenance of the present discriminatory system. Its elimination raises the "spectre" of daily and neighborly contacts across racial lines. Hence, of all the forms of discrimination, it is among the most resistant to change. But, by the same reasoning, changes in residential segregation can be expected to have the greatest effect on the total system of discrimination. The problem, then, is to engineer a revolution in Negro-white relations. It is hoped that this theoretical study will contribute to that aim.

With respect to the second aim, our object is to illustrate the potential of computer simulation for sociology. Computer simulation allows the manipulation of large sets of variables that are interrelated in very complicated ways. It is, therefore, a powerful aid in building sociological theory.

It is likely that in the future computer simulation will play an increasingly important part in sociological research. Hopefully, this illustration will serve to interest some readers in its potential.

Our debt to others is great. First, we are indebted to University College of Syracuse University, particularly to Dean Clifford Winters, for providing the financial support which made our work possible. In addition, support for a great deal of computer time was provided by a National Science Foundation Grant, GP - 1137.

Many of our friends and colleagues have made helpful suggestions during the course of this project. Outstanding among these are Syracuse University Professors Max Bloom, Ronald Ridker, Sakari Jutila, Richard Videbeck and Thomas J. Fararo, Robert McGinnis of Cornell University, Ronald Corwin of N. Y. U., and Kiyoshi Ikeda of Oberlin College. Mrs. Barbara Rumsey, a real estate agent, has been extremely helpful in providing insights, as have Roland Werner, William Alexander, John Pilger, Sue Freeman and Charles Raymond, all former associates at the Systems Research Committee at Syracuse University.

The background bibliographic work was done by Satish Sheth and Helen Weldon. Roland Werner wrote much of the computer program, and John Pilger collaborated in deriving the segregation index.

LINTON C. FREEMAN
MORRIS H. SUNSHINE

Honolulu, Hawaii and Kent, Ohio
May 15, 1970

1. Introduction

1.1 The Need for Theory

The study of ethnic relations—particularly Negro-white relations—is a subject of consuming interest to American social scientists. In fact, a recent bibliography lists over 3,500 books and articles on Negro-white relations published between 1954 and 1966.[1]

As a result of all this interest we have learned a great deal about the attitudes toward and life-chances of minority groups. In recent years research designs have become increasingly sophisticated, and the number of established generalizations about ethnic relations has grown.[2]

Relatively little attention, however, has been given to the task of organizing these generalizations together into systematic interrelated sets, or theories. Without such organization it is difficult to use even well established generalizations to make predictions or to devise solutions to practical problems. Empirical research is inherently descriptive; it is only when its generalizations are tied together into theories that we can go beyond the "facts" to make useful inferences.

The present research was designed, therefore, as a first step toward building a theory of ethnic residential segregation. No questionnaires were administered; no interviews were conducted; in fact no data were collected at all. Instead, an attempt was made to organize some generalizations about patterns of ethnic housing.

1

1.2   Strategies for Building Theory

In sociology the word "theory" has many meanings. It is sometimes used to characterize the results of casual—though often insightful—speculation in the absence of data. Sometimes it suggests the irate commentary of social critics, and sometimes even the verbal description of empirical events. With increasing frequency, however, "theory" is used in sociology in the sense it is intended here: as a systematic set of definitions and empirical descriptions linked together by means of an explicit formal structure.[3]

The formal structure of a theory includes a set of initial propositions (axioms) and definitions together with their attendant theorems and corollaries. Every assertion is either given immediately as an axiom or is deductible from the axioms and definitions. Thus, the generalizations of theoretical knowledge form a hierarchy in which many special descriptions are logically derived from a small number of highly general propositions.[4]

Currently, there are two available strategies for building formal theories: (1) mathematical derivation, and (2) simulation. Strict mathematical derivation provides a powerful tool for the development of theory. Theories generated by such formal procedures are clear, concise, often elegant, and they can take advantage of the vast structure of formal thought that is modern mathematics. Such theories, however, are by necessity, often rather simplistic. The rigorous derivation of even a single theorem in a mathematical system of any complexity may involve years of work. For the complex problems that characterize much of sociology, such proofs are beset with immense difficulties. A great number of simplifying assumptions are often necessary; so many, in fact, that mathematical theories are frequently accused—justifiably—of lack of realism. In the long run, of course, the tools of mathematics can provide a method for gradually increasing the complexity, and therefore the realism, of theories. For the solution of immediate practical problems however, such strict mathematical systems are usually unsatisfactory.

Computer simulation provides an attractive alternative to strict mathematical derivation. The postulates of a formal system—all the variables and relations—are programmed into a computer, along with a set of specific conditions that function as additional particularizing assumptions. The programmed machine then becomes an analogue model of the phenomenon of concern; it obeys the general principles laid out in the axioms. Like strict mathematical procedures, computer simulations generate deductions.

The deductions generated by a computer simulation, however, are deductions of a peculiar sort: they are restricted to the case specified by the conditions of the particularizing assumptions. Thus, a strict mathematical derivation would involve the manipulation of abstract symbols; it might include a step like:
let
$$a + (-b) = c,$$
and
$$a = b,$$
therefore, by the rules of ordinary algebra,
$$c = 0.$$
The corresponding step in a computer simulation would involve additional assumptions like the following:
let
$$a = b = 4,$$
or let
$$a = b = 257.$$
Then, given the expression,
$$a + (-b) = c,$$
we get, in the first case,
$$c = 4 + (-4) = 0,$$
and in the second case
$$c = 257 + (-257) = 0 .$$
Note that in the simulation we provide no general proof of the expression
$$c = 0.$$
Instead, we simply show that for certain particular values of a and b, c does indeed turn out to be zero. This illustration is, of course, extremely trivial. Simulation would hardly be needed in such a simple problem. But this same particularizing device characterizes simulation in the complex problems where it is applied. In general, then, simulation does not yield the general abstract solutions of strict mathematical analysis; the solutions provided by the computer are particular results that depend upon the assumed conditions of a given experiment.

This is the same procedure as that used by engineers to study the aerodynamic properties of a model aircraft in a wind tunnel. One can examine the aerodynamic characteristics of a whole range of basic wing design without ever determining the general abstract relationship between the form of wings and, say, stability in flight. It is necessary only to try the particular designs of interest. Such experiments do, indeed, lack the elegance and generality of abstract derivations, but they do provide immediate solutions to practical problems, and often they point in the direction in which general solutions might be sought.

When compared with mathematical derivation, then, simulation is somewhat limiting. There is, however, a compensatory advantage: simulation permits the solution of extremely complex sets of equations. Simulation will tolerate a degree of complexity that cannot even be approached by ordinary mathematics.[5] Ithiel de Sola Pool has characterized computer simulation as:

". . . a massive breakthrough for the social sciences, for it offers a way of simultaneously considering the vast number of variables—social and physical, continuous and discontinuous—all of which interact in a real social situation."[6]

Simulation, therefore, may be viewed as a technique which aids in solving theoretical problems for complex social situations. It is no substitute for formal mathematical procedures but it is a step in the direction of theoretical rigor. If nothing else, simulation can reveal whether a set of axioms will yield derivations that are at all reasonable in the light of existing information. Thus, it may be used for the first steps in building theory; it is often useful, before even attempting the formal solution of an axiom set, to see if its deductions are "in the right ball park." Such a system may be simulated, and modified until it is reasonable before formal derivation is pursued.

Simulation also helps to clarify our thinking about theoretical matters. In order to write a computer program it is necessary to specify our variables and relations precisely. The computer tolerates absolutely no ambiguity. It often happens, therefore, that an expression that seems to be well defined—one that could pass in descriptive sociology—turns out to be fuzzy. In the process of writing computer programs all this hidden ambiguity is forcibly revealed.

A corollary of this result is the fact that the organization of axioms into simulation programs tends also to reveal areas where data are missing. The development of a simulation program involves the specification of numerical values for all relevant variables. In many cases it turns out that existing data are insufficient for this task. Thus, in writing a program, the attention of the theorist is focused on areas of incomplete empirical information.

In short, computer simulation affords a powerful and convenient tool for building theory. Factual data suggest that under certain conditions important relations hold among a set of variables. A computer is programmed to reflect these constant conditions of parameters as well as the relevant variables and relations. This program governs the behavior of the computer and initiates a process in which the values taken by the variables may change. These changes are observed and, when possible, compared with changes observed in a natural setting. The set of governing variables and relations may be revised until any desired degree of correspondence is established. Thus, the programmed computer serves as a model of the phenomena under study. In this fashion simulation may be used to build theory, and theory built in this manner has some hope of tolerating enough complexity to be useful in the solution of practical problems.

1.3 A Theory of Ethnic Residence

The problem of organizing current knowledge about patterns of ethnic residence is not a simple one. Rose has made the point that,

"While examples of racial, religious, and ethnic intolerance are readily observed, the forces which serve to create, maintain, perpetuate, and alleviate intergroup tensions are highly complex."[7]

In view of this apparent complexity, computer simulation was chosen as the appropriate strategy for building a preliminary theory of ethnic residence.

The empirical literature on housing and segregation was reviewed, and the generalizations of that literature provided the basic building blocks for the proposed theory. The first part of the theory refers to the general housing market. It is presented in Chapters 2 and 3. This general housing market model was developed to provide a base-line context into which ethnic factors could later be introduced. In Chapters 5 and 6 variables referring to ethnicity are appended to the market model. It is hoped that in this manner the precise effects of factors related to ethnicity will be uncovered.

The theory proposed here is preliminary. It stands in need of considerable refinement before it can be used to engineer social change. It is, however, a self-conscious step toward that goal.

[1]E. W. Miller, *The Negro in America: A Bibliography,* Cambridge, Massachusetts: Harvard University Press, 1966.

[2]See G. E. Simpson and J. M. Yinger, *Racial and Cultural Minorities,* New York: Harper and Row, Revised Edition, 1958, B. Berlson and G. A. Steiner, *Human Behavior: An Inventory of Scientific Findings,* New York: Harcourt, Brace and World, 1964, and P. I. Rose, *They and We,* New York: Random House, 1964 for recent reviews of these generalizations.

[3]R. McGinnis, *Mathematical Foundations for Social Analysis,* Indianapolis: Bobbs-Merrill, 1965.

[4]R. B. Braithwaite, *Scientific Explanation,* New York: Harper and Brothers (Harper Torchbooks), 1960.

[5]J. S. Coleman, *Introduction to Mathematical Sociology,* Glencoe, Illinois: Free Press, 1964.

[6]I. de Sola Pool, "Simulating social systems," *International Science and Technology* (March, 1964), 62-70.

[7]P. I. Rose, *op. cit.,* p. 4.

2. The Neighborhood Housing Market Process

The patterning of ethnic residential segregation takes place within the context of a housing market. The interplay between market conditions and individual decisions influences house-selling and house-buying activities and may, in turn, affect the spatial distribution of minorities in residential areas. It was deemed necessary, therefore, to develop a model for a general neighborhood housing market process to provide a context into which ethnic constraints could be introduced. It is this general market that is described in the present chapter. Consideration of the complications arising from the introduction of ethnic factors will be delayed until Chapter 5.

2.1 Time

This theory of ethnic residence is dynamic. It is intended to describe and explain changes in patterns of residence through time. All relations proposed in the current theory are, therefore, expressed as events occurring with the passage of time.

The basic unit of time in the theory as it now stands is a cycle. A cycle begins with the event of each home owner deciding whether or not to put his house on the market and ends with the event of each owner of an unsold house on the market deciding how much to reduce his asking price.

As a time measure a cycle is an arbitrary unit; it is convenient

7

for ordering events. Currently not enough is known about the
housing market to establish a correspondence between a cycle
and any unit of real time. In the long run it is probably possible
to find such a correspondence. When this is done, the result will
undoubtedly have a stochastic element; one cycle will not correspond to a standard unit like a week or a month, but to an
expectation. Thus, a given cycle may, for example, correspond
to two weeks or three weeks, or even six weeks, but the most
likely period would be, say, four weeks. In this case, most cycles
would be fairly close to the expected length of real time, but
they would vary around this expectation—some longer, some
shorter—in a random way. In any case, the current unit of time
in this theory is the cycle.

2.2 A Neighborhood Housing Market

The economist who specializes in housing market analysis may
refer to a contiguous physical area which is more or less well-
bounded as a local housing market area.[1] A housing market area
is a physical area within which all dwelling units are substitutable;
they are all in competition for a purchaser through a price
mechanism. The physical boundaries of a local housing market
area are fuzzy and subject to change. They are given by the
outlook of the potential buyer: which dwellings are effectively
competing for his housing dollar? The core of the difficulty in
fixing boundaries lies in determining the inter-substitutability of
units. Are multiple-family dwelling units substitutable for single-
family units? Is a house in New York City substitutable for a
house in San Francisco? In the latter case, it is perfectly clear
that a job-holding buyer would not be indifferent between
locating in New York and San Francisco and that houses in these
two cities are not in the same housing market.

In developing our model of the housing market we resolved
the problem of defining boundaries by means of a series of five
simplifying assumptions. First, every vacant house is considered
to be for sale; there are no rentals in our economy. Second, each
house that is up for sale competes with all of the others in the
market by means of a price mechanism; there is only one market
in the model. Third, every house is considered to be a single
family dwelling unit; from the structural standpoint they are

substitutable.   Fourth, the houses are assumed to be generally of
the same quality; we do not distinguish between old and new,
well-kept and run-down.   Fifth, the space is "small;" buyers are
assumed not to have directional preferences.

We are dealing, essentially, with a single neighborhood market.
Urban sociologists have written a great deal about "neighborhoods," and, though the concept is somewhat vague, it is usually
taken to refer to a bounded region containing persons who are
both fairly homogeneous in socio-economic characteristics, and
connected by bonds of mutual recognition through social inter-
course.   In general, sociologists would agree to call an area a
neighborhood if many of the residents of the area have close
inter-personal relations with others in that area, if local organ-
izations flourish, if there is a fairly high degree of moral consensus
concerning standards of behavior, and if residents of the area
see themselves as socially similar.[2]   It is these facets of the social
organization of an area which distinguish a neighborhood from
an arbitrary statistical entity like a census tract or the local
economic market previously mentioned.

Well-established neighborhoods have clearly defined boundaries.
These are established through communication and consensus.
Frequently, these boundaries fall along main transportation routes
or along other topographical lines.   Residents of such a neighborhood are sensitive to intra-neighborhood events—the leveling of
the old grammar school, the sale of the synagogue to the Baptists,
the sewer problem after a heavy rain—and they may be quite
indifferent to events occurring nearby because those events occur
outside of the bounds of their neighborhood.   It is usually the
case, especially where neighborhoods have traditional names as in
Chicago, that nearby outsiders as well as insiders are able to
define the boundaries of a given neighborhood.

Neighborhoods vary of course, and a great deal of social research shows that certain residential areas would not meet the
criteria for "neighborhood" given above.   Specifically, deteriorated
portions of the city near the central business district seem to be
populated with persons who are relatively indifferent to each other
and local institutions, and who have no sentimental ties to the
area.   Such regions have relatively high population turnover, a
low degree of moral consensus and the scope of community concern is quite small.

Our model housing market is assumed to be a well-established neighborhood. It is a rectangular area made up of 24 blocks. Each block contains 10 single-family dwellings; see Figure 2.1. Residents are assumed to have a degree of community awareness and concern. The assumption is reflected in three properties of the theoretical model. First, the residential space is well bounded; residents have consensus on neighborhood boundaries. Second, all residents are sensitive to experimentally pertinent events occurring anywhere in the space. Third, in keeping with the concept of an established neighborhood, we assume a state of moral consensus with respect to certain collective acts.

This third assumption allows us to define variables for the neighborhood as a unit. Prejudice, for example, is used primarily as an attribute of individual households, but in addition, mean prejudice level for the neighborhood as a whole is used in determining the probability of organized community action in the face of an ethnic "threat." Organized acts of this sort require consensus—they can occur only when some basis for consensus exists—only when a neighborhood is established. In summary, we construe the residential model space as a special kind of transactional arena—one having the properties of a neighborhood.

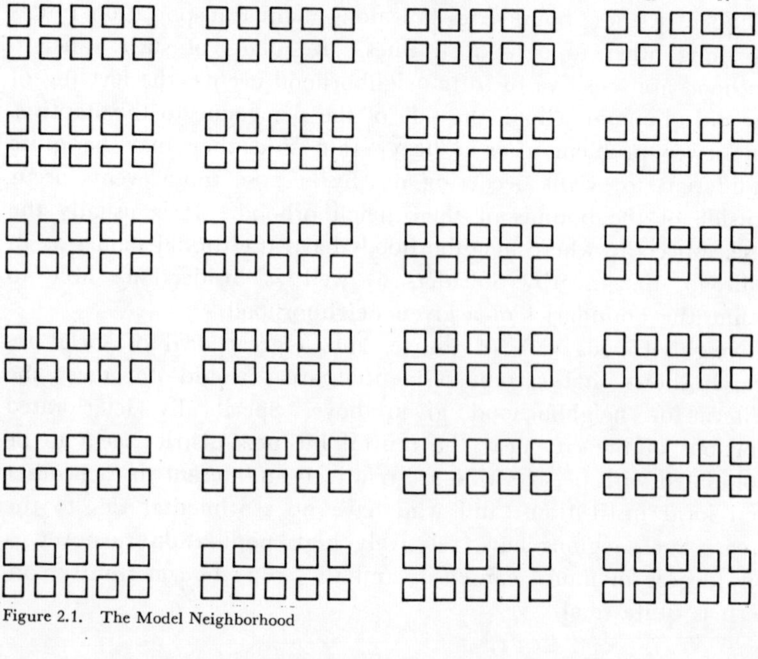

Figure 2.1. The Model Neighborhood

2.3   Initiating the Market Process: Neighborhood Out-migration

The initiation of the neighborhood housing market process requires that people decide to sell their houses and move out of the neighborhood. Why do people move out of a neighborhood? The full story is very complicated. Rossi, in fact, requires several hundred pages to explore the motivational bases for moving.[3] Here, all that need be noted are the most salient features of this decision-making process.

There are many factors that might initiate a decision to leave a house and search for a new one. These factors derive from a person's dissatisfactions with: (1) the size or layout of a house, (2) the facilities (like wiring and heating) of the house, (3) its location with respect to work, friends, shopping, and so on, (4) the physical environment of the area (smoke, noise, and the like), (5) the social environment, and (6) housing cost.

The reproduction of these sorts of personal factors and the attempt to generalize the decision-making process underlying house selling is beyond the scope of this project. For present purposes, however, there is no need to attempt such a generalization. We can reproduce the results of the process of decision to sell without being concerned with details of the operation of that process.

In the model neighborhood the decision to put a house on the market was defined as a random process. At the start of the market process, and periodically thereafter, each occupied house has an opportunity to go on the market with a small constant probability. These probabilities are independent and equal for all occupied houses. Thus, although a person may decide to sell his house for any of a number of reasons, this variation is irrelevant in the present model.

The use of a random process in this context depends upon two assumptions. First, under normal circumstances, the variation in the number of houses vacated in a neighborhood during a given period of time is fairly small. Some seasonal variation may occur, but, barring an industrial closing or an urban renewal project, the tendency to move out will be reasonably stable. Second, there are in general no appreciable spatial biases in the tendency to sell houses within a small neighborhood. Selling is not contagious; the decision to move is conditioned only to a very small degree, if at all, by the decisions of neighbors to leave or stay. On the basis of these assumptions, then, we have defined a parameter, α, the probability that each occupied house will go on the market at any time cycle. This parameter may differ from neighborhood to neighborhood, but it is expected to remain constant in a single neighborhood, at least for relatively short periods of time.

2.4 Setting the Initial Selling Price

Once the decision has been made to put a house on the market, an initial asking price must be determined. For many sellers this may pose a dilemma: in a competitive market there may be a discrepancy between the price they would like to get (on the basis of investment, replacement costs, or the desire to make a large profit) and the current market price for comparable houses. In view of this personal conflict it was necessary to define a variable and a parameter for this process: pricing average and the acquisitiveness distribution.

Pricing average, y, is a variable used to set the lower limit of the initial asking price. It serves as a "reality principle" and tends to keep the market stable. It is simply the mean of the prices at which the last ten houses in the neighborhood were sold. Since all houses in the model neighborhood are considered to be comparable, this averaging device is essentially the same as that used by agents and appraisers in setting house values. At the start of each experiment this variable is initially set at any realistic value.

Acquisitiveness is defined as a dispositional attribute of individuals. It is assumed that each person has a more or less stable tendency to be economically acquisitive.[4]

The concept of acquisitiveness corresponds rather closely to the classical economist's conception of the profit motive, and it has some overlap with Murray's Need Acquisition.[5] The highly acquisitive person is preoccupied with money and with its acquisition. A person low in acquisitiveness thinks little about money and it not concerned with economic gain.

Perhaps the best way of clarifying this concept is to define it in terms of the marginal utility of money.[6] For a highly acquisitive person extra dollars always have high utility, while for the person at the opposite extreme, extra dollars are of relatively little consequence.

Little is known about the distribution of this trait. For present purposes it is expressed in a scale containing five ordered classes:

$$v = 0, 1, 2, 3, 4.$$

Since its distribution form is unknown, several arbitrarily selected distributions were tried.

Table 2.1 Selected Distributions of Acquisitiveness.

γ	Probability that v equals				
	0	1	2	3	4
0	.2400	.4120	.2650	.0760	.0080
1	.0625	.2500	.3750	.2500	.0625
2	.0080	.0760	.2650	.4120	.2400

A particular form is chosen by parameter, γ, according to Table 2.1. The value of γ sets the probability of each possible level of acquisitiveness for any person.

These variables, pricing average and acquisitiveness, are used to determine the initial price. An increment is defined according to the acquisitiveness of the seller. Then this increment is used to determine the degree to which the pricing average is inflated in setting the initial price. This relation is expressed in the following equation:

$$\text{Initial price} = n_0 = y + .025\, vy, \tag{2.1}$$

where the numerical constant, .025, controls the degree to which acquisitiveness may inflate the initial asking price. Thus, more acquisitive sellers tend to ask relatively more than less acquisitive ones. Sellers who rate 0 in acquisitiveness simply ask the going price. This equation is used to set initial prices on all houses that go on the market.

2.5 The Buyer

The next phase in the market process requires the appearance of a buyer. The motivation for buying a house turns around the buyer's dissatisfaction with his current housing. These matters have already been discussed.

In general, the number of buyers in the housing market fluctuates with economic conditions. In the microcosm of the present theory, however, it was necessary to assume stability of general

economic conditions. For the relatively short periods of time
with which we are dealing, this assumption is probably not too
unrealistic. In any case we have assumed a fixed number of
families seeking to buy a house during each cycle of time. This
number, λ, is a parameter in the theory.

In order to buy a house, a potential buyer needs money. It is
an obvious fact that buyers can only buy houses that they can
afford. Their purchasing power derives from their income, savings and access to credit. These three aspects of purchasing
power, however, are interrelated so that person with a small
income have small savings and can command small loans. Purchasing power, therefore, is distributed in the same general form
as income.

A good deal of attention has been devoted to the study of
income distributions. These studies are summarized by Aitchison
and Brown who conclude that the lognormal is the most suitable
distribution for the description of income.[7] The lognormal is a
unimodal distribution with a concentration of frequencies at the
low end. See Figure 2.2. For this analysis, then, the variable
w, purchasing power, was assumed to be lognormally distributed.

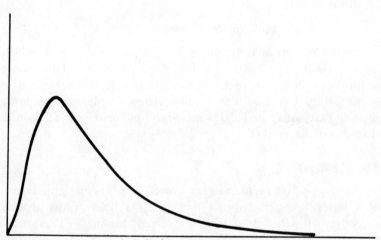

Figure 2.2.   A Frequency Curve of a Lognormal Distribution

This assumption requires the introduction of two parameters, μ and σ, which define the distribution. Together, these parameters determine the probability that a buyer has any given purchasing power. This purchasing power sets an upper limit on the buyer's field of eligible houses.

Realism necessitates that there be a lower limit on this field as well. There is a demonstrable correlation between income and the amount spent on housing.[8] For example, a person whose style of life calls for and who can realistically afford a $30,000 house is unlikely to buy a $5,000 one. That, in a social sense, would be unfitting. Consequently, we have postulated that houses will be considered only when they fall within some fixed range. The range is established by setting a lower price limit that is proportionately less than purchasing power:

$$\text{Lower price limit} = w - .2w.$$

Thus we have defined both an upper and a lower bound, between which a buyer must find a house.

2.6 The Transaction

Between the buyer's two price limits there may be a number of possible houses. The cost of the houses being considered is important to buyers and apparently they do try to optimize. The optimizing process involves balancing cost against the exterior appearance of the house, its size and the neighborhood as a social environment. As between two or more generally acceptable dwelling units, the cheaper one is chosen.[9]

A transaction occurs when the buyer meets the seller's price or the seller's price meets the buyer's offer. In practice, price is negotiable and the process is characterized by bluffs and counterbluffs. The buyer makes a low offer; the seller reduces his price a little in order to entice the buyer to make a higher offer, and so on. The details of this complex process are beyond the scope of this theory.[10]

Here, the process is simplified. In the first place, we are dealing with a homogenous neighborhood; the houses are maximally similar in all respects but price. This means that the buyer may choose simply on the basis of price. Furthermore, the negotiation process has been truncated. Each seller has a current asking price, and each buyer has a price range within which he must operate. If the buyer can meet the asking price of any seller, a transaction will occur. If more than one house falls within the buyer's range he will buy the cheapest.

2.7 Readjusting the Selling Price

The last step in each cycle of the marketing process—the step that ends a time cycle—is the adjustment of seller's asking price.

Anyone who has ever tried to sell his house knows that the process can be painful. It may be on the market for weeks or months, and the seller may spend a great deal of time and psychic energy showing the house to prospects who thereafter disappear. The usual alternative to this unhappy state of affairs is to reduce the selling price. Ordinarily, this simple strategy increases the likelihood of its sale. However, if the decrement is too small the probability of selling is not really enhanced; if it is too large the house will surely sell but the economic loss would be great.

Here again, as in the case of setting the initial selling price, acquisitiveness comes into play. The role of acquisitiveness in setting this decrement, however, is somewhat ambiguous. On one hand, the highly acquisitive person should be willing to suffer great personal inconvenience (repeatedly showing the house, negotiating, and so on) in order to get the maximum price. On the other hand, such a person would be unwilling to suffer the accumulative losses resulting from tying up his capital in, and paying taxes on, an unsold house. Data relevant to this dilemma are unavailable, so a more or less arbitrary choice was made. We reasoned that the highly acquisitive person would aim for a quick sale in order to reinvest his capital in a profit making venture. His interest loss in prolonged deferment of sale in addition to the costs of taxes and assessments would, we felt, tip the scale. Highly acquisitive persons were, therefore, assigned a quick sale strategy. The equation for the decremented asking price is

$$\text{Decremented Price} = n_{i+1} = n_i - .005 \, v \, n_i, \qquad (2.2)$$

where $n_i =$ the previous asking price at the ith cycle.

This, then, is the basic model of a neighborhood housing economy. It is, at this point, somewhat crude and oversimplified, and it often depends upon untested assumptions. But it is a step in the right direction. It specifies a series of axioms—each plausible—and thereby defines the rules for a sequence of inter-personal acts. These acts define a process with observable consequences. We can, for example, observe vacancy rates, price trends, and entrance rates as they result from different values of the input parameters. That we shall do in the next chapter.

[1]C. Rapkin, L. Winnick and D. M. Blank, *Housing Market Analysis, A Study of Theory and Methods,* Washington: U.S. Government Printing Office.

[2]P. H. Rossi, *Why People Move,* Glencoe, Illinois: Free Press, 1955.

[3]*Ibid.*

[4]P. A. Samuelson, "A note on the measurement of utility," *Review of Economic Studies,* 4 (1937), 155-161.

[5]For the economist's view see D.C. McClelland, *The Achieving Society,* Princeton, New Jersey: Van Nostrand, 1961, and for the psychologist's view see H. A. Murray (ed.), *Explorations in Personality,* New York: Oxford University Press, 1938.

[6]P. A. Samuelson, *Economics, and Introductory Analysis,* New York: McGraw-Hill, 1948, and W. Vickrey, "Measuring marginal utility by reaction to risk," *Econometrica,* 13 (1945), 319-333.

[7]J. Aitchison and J. A. C. Brown, *The Lognormal Distribution,* Cambridge: Cambridge University Press, 1957.

[8]*Ibid.*

[9]P. H. Rossi, *op. cit.,* p. 165. -

[10]T. C. Schelling, "An Essay on Bargaining," *American Economic Review,* 46 (1965), 281-306.

3. Simulation of the Neighborhood Housing Market

Normally, the market for housing is competitive and the price level is determined by countless individual decisions as they are dictated by supply and demand factors. The relationship between supply and demand is indicated by the number of unsold houses in the neighborhood. If we hold the number of buyers constant, it follows that an increase in unsold houses implies an increase in supply and a weakening in demand; similarly, a decrease in the number of unsold houses means a decrease in supply and a strengthening in demand. And, according to the conventions of classical economic theory, an excess of supply arrests price increases, and a decrease in supply encourages price increases.

The market in this model is governed by five parameters: (1) α, the probability of a house being placed on the market, (2) γ, the distribution of acquisitiveness of sellers, (3) λ, the number of persons applying for housing at each time cycle, and (4) and (5) μ and σ, the parameters governing the distribution of buyer purchasing power.

The effect of each of these quantities for the operation of the market can only be determined by examining the relations among them. The number of buyers, for example, has market significance only in terms of the number of sellers. It is clear that if the probability of leaving is set at a very small value and at the

18

same time the number seeking housing is set at a rather large value, there will be an excess of demand over supply and a seller's market will obtain; prices will, therefore, rise. Similarly, if the parameters are arranged so that there are many more sellers than buyers, this will exercise a depressive effect on housing values, and a buyer's market will prevail. Furthermore, we can control the rapidity with which the price level changes through the seller fiscal acquisitiveness parameter. If this is set at a large value and a seller's market obtains, the price level will move up quickly; on the other hand, if it is a buyer's market, that setting of the parameter will depress prices quickly.

From these remarks it should be clear that the model does not involve the direct manipulation of house prices, except in the trivial sense of setting the initial cost of housing. Rather, we control supply through the probability of selling and fiscal acquisitiveness, and control demand through the number of applicants for housing, their purchasing power, and their range to the low bid. The number of unsold houses on the market and the price level of houses sold are outputs.

In order to examine how the axioms of the model govern sales and prices the market has been simulated under various experimental conditions. The results of the experiments are discussed below.

3.1 The Normal Housing Market

For most market conditions, the relationship between the number of unsold houses on the market and the average price of sales follows the form shown in Figure 3.1. The graph shows in pictorial form how the market operates under usual supply-demand conditions. The straight horizontal line represents the average for the two quantities, price and number of vacancies. The dynamic aspect of the relationship is given by reading from left to right.

The relation of these curves to each other conveys the usual supply-demand and price relations. When the number of unsold houses is below normal, a relatively low supply is indicated, and prices ascend. As the vacancy rate rises and approaches its mean there is a retardation in the rate at which house prices increase. Then, as the vacancy rate reaches its mean, prices are stabilized.

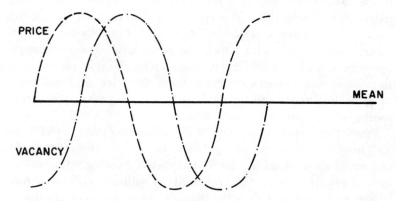

Figure 3.1. The Relationship between Price and Vacancy

Continuing, the graph shows that when the vacancy rate rises above its mean, prices turn down and do not begin to ascend again until the vacancy rate reaches, passes and starts to go below its mean. In short, whenever the vacancy rate is below its mean, prices ascend; whenever, the vacancy rate is above the mean, prices descend; and, whenever the vacancy rate is at the mean, prices are steady. Similarly, whenever prices fall below the average, more buyers are attracted and the vacancy rate decreases. And whenever prices go above their mean, buyers are repelled and the vacancy rate ascends. Finally, when house prices hit their mean, the vacancy rate stabilizes.

The vertical and horizontal dimensions of the graph are not calibrated because no correspondence is intended between the concept of a normal market and particular values for vacancy rate and price. There are an infinite number of graphs which may vary in mean, amplitude and frequency but which display the essential relations described here. Insofar as this is so, the set of such graphs corresponds to our notion of the normal market. It should be noted that Figure 3.1 is based on experimental data that exhibit considerable fluctuation and that these curves have been smoothed. This is, then, an idealized relation.

Figures 3.2 and 3.3 show a concrete illustration of a normal market. The magnitudes of the experimental parameters are given. The expression "Probability of Leaving" refers to the probability of a house being vacated and put on the market at each cycle. For this experiment, this probability is set at .01 which means that each occupied house is vacated at the beginning of each cycle with a probability of .01. When all 240 houses are occupied this yields an expected number of houses vacated of 2.4 per cycle.

"Number Seeking Housing" refers to the absolute number of persons looking for, but not necessarily buying, houses at each cycle. In this first experiment 10 potential buyers are assumed to seek housing in this neighborhood at each cycle.

In this first series of experiments the "Acquisitiveness" parameter was handled in a special way. Instead of using a distribution on this trait, we assigned each individual buyer an acquisitiveness score of 4. Acquisitiveness, then, was not varied either from person to person or from experiment to experiment in this series.

The distribution of "Purchasing Power" is lognormal. The mean and standard deviation of the underlying normal variate are not shown, but they are 9.75 and .50 respectively. These values yield a lognormal distribution of purchasing power expressed in dollars. Its mean is $17,150.

Finally, the initial selling price is set at $15,000. This is an arbitrary setting; it was chosen merely to get the marketing process started. Once underway, the market will find its own price level based upon supply and demand factors.

Figures 3.2 and 3.3. Simulated "Normal" Market

PROBABILITY OF LEAVING	.01
NUMBER SEEKING HOUSING	10
ACQUISITIVENESS*	
PURCHASING POWER MEAN	17150.

* Acquisitiveness was set at 4 uniformly for all sellers during this experiment.

The output of the market process is shown in the figures. Figure 3.2 shows the variation in price levels throughout the course of this experiment. And Figure 3.3 shows the total num-

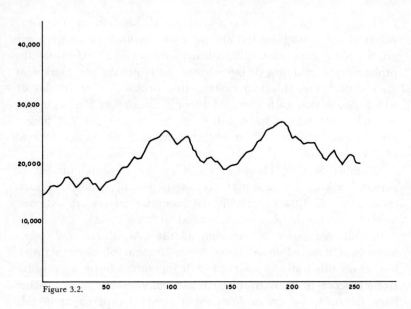

Figure 3.2.

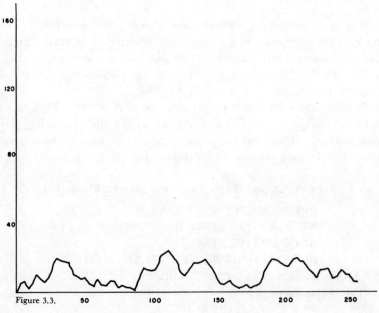

Figure 3.3.

ber of houses on the market. Further details of this process are
shown in Table 1 in Appendix A. The columns of Table 1
reveal the numeric values for relevant variables in the experi-

ment. The column headed "Exit Rate" shows the number of houses put on the market. The column headed "Entrance Rate" reveals the number of houses purchased. The "Total Vacant" column is based on the exit and entrance data and gives a moment-by-moment account of the number of unsold houses on the market. The "Average Cost" column gives the average cost of houses sold at that cycle. The last column, "Pricing Average," gives the average cost for the ten most recently sold houses irrespective of cycle.

There is a sufficient amount of demand in this neighborhood as indicated by the ratio of sellers to applicants to generate a gentle, longrun increase in the price level. However, the system possesses the earmarks of a normal market. For example, the low vacancy entries through cycles 50-90 on Figure 3.3 indicate a temporary strengthening in demand and this is associated with a corresponding rise in prices in Figure 3.2. Thereafter, through cycles 90-150, we observe the effects of this price increase: prices are "too high," demand falls off (note the higher values in Figure 3.3), and prices turn downward. The pattern is repeated showing the typical shifting equilibrium with an average price in the range from $21,000 to $22,000 and an average number of vacancies in the range from 8 to 15.

3.2 The Ghost Town

In a changing society, neighborhoods—even whole towns—are sometimes abandoned completely. Changing patterns of industrialization and basic shifts in the economy may lead to such upheavals. The mining towns of Colorado and Southern Illinois and some mill towns of New England are examples. In such cases supply greatly outruns demand and the dynamic equilibrium model does not hold.

We can simulate such an imbalance between supply and demand by modifying our input parameters. Figures 3.4 and 3.5 (and Table 2 in the Appendix) show a case where the exit probability is doubled.

When these figures are compared with Figures 3.2 and 3.3, it will be seen that the ratio of sellers to applicants for housing has been doubled. This has the effect of increasing supply and weakening demand. The consequences are shown most dramatically in the number of houses on the market; the values

steadily build up from 0 to 173. And, as the axioms of the
model dictate, the price level falls steadily. Furthermore, it will
never fluctuate around a stable mean as in the case of the
normal market.

This market "crisis" however, is not due entirely to the buyer-
seller ratio. The acquisitiveness and price-to-low-bid parameters
also make a contribution to the economic situation. The acquisitiveness parameter leads to the reduction of the prices of unsold
houses at every time cycle. As the general price level falls, the
operation of the range to low bid parameter eventuates in a
smaller number of houses falling into the affordable-acceptable
set, and this leads to the further reduction of sales. In other
words, the main source of the crisis lies in the excess of sellers

Figures 3.4 and 3.5. Simulated Ghost Town Market

PROBABILITY OF LEAVING   .02
NUMBER SEEKING HOUSING   10
ACQUISITIVENESS*
PURCHASING POWER MEAN   17150.

* Acquisitiveness was set at 4 uniformly for all sellers during
  this experiment.

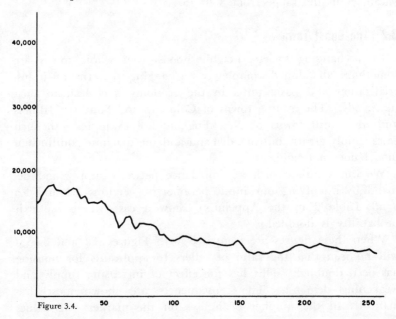

Figure 3.4.

over buyers, but the crisis is deepened by the seller's urge to sell and the unwillingness of buyers with that income distribution to buy such "cheap" housing.

It sometimes happens that a drop in neighborhood property values is associated with a change in the social composition of the inhabitants of the neighborhood. However, this experiment does not simulate the pattern of invasion and succession. What we are observing here is the death of the area; it is being systematically depopulated. All one can say is that the fall in prices should make it attractive to buyers, but, speaking figuratively, the neighborhood is so altogether unattractive that virtually no one will buy a house there at any price.

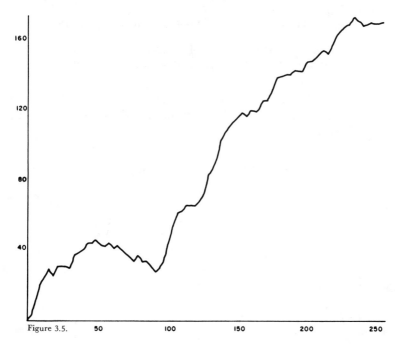

Figure 3.5.

3.3 The Boom Town

A changing society is sometimes characterized also by the explosive growth of a community. The most extreme example in our history probably occurred during the California gold rush. But industrial towns often exhibit periods of rapid growth.

This simulated "boom town" phenomenon is shown in Figures 3.6 and 3.7 (and in Table 3 in the Appendix), by a sharp in-

crease in the number of persons seeking housing. This value is
increased by a factor of five (from 10 to 50) over previous experiments. This experiment, then, is a study in high demand.

Strong demand forces prices up. The average cost column
indicates that this market will achieve stability in the range of
$38,000-$42,000, an impressive growth in property values. However, this neighborhood housing market is more similar to the
normal market than to the ghost town. It has a point of dynamic
equilibrium: when prices go "too high"—beyond the range of the
distribution of purchasing power—the vacancy rate increases, demand slackens and prices come down. Not to the low level of
the initial price, but they do come down. Similarly, as the price

Figures 3.6 and 3.7. Simulated Boom Town Market

PROBABILITY OF LEAVING   .01
NUMBER SEEKING HOUSING   50
ACQUISITIVENESS*
PURCHASING POWER MEAN   17150.

* Acquisitiveness was set at 4 uniformly for all sellers during
this experiment.

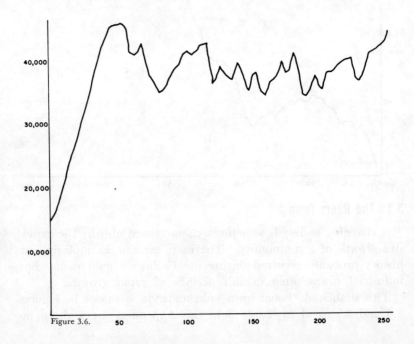

Figure 3.6.

level falls, more applicants can actually buy, the vacancy rate falls, and the price decline is slowed. In other words, the graph of this market shows the wave form of Figure 3.2 and 3.3. This market is unusual only in the magnitude of the great differential between the initial price and final equilibrium price.

As in the preceding experiments, the acquisitiveness parameter leads to the regular revision of prices of unsold houses downward, but demand is very strong and houses are seldom on the market for an appreciable length of time: the moment prices come into the range of purchasing power, the houses are snapped up. Acquisitiveness, in these circumstances, can only temporarily mitigate the fluctuation in prices. In a word, the real key to the economic situation is the ratio of buyers to sellers and the purchasing power distribution of buyers.

Many other experiments could be presented here in order to display further how the axioms of the model govern a competitive market. However, this small sample of output shows that the model establishes sensible relations between supply and demand factors and property values. And while the model does not systematically incorporate all the conceptual attributes of the classical free marketplace, the output is consistent with the usual assumptions of rationality, completeness of information, and independence of individual decision-making.

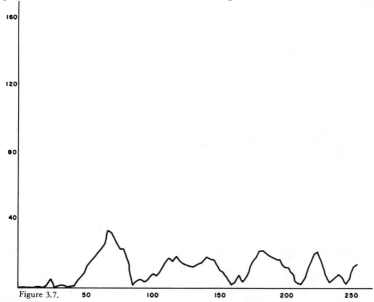

Figure 3.7.

In closing this chapter, a minor word of caution may be warranted. The columnar entries in these tables must be taken as statistical estimate. In other words, if an experiment is replicated the two outputs will not be identical. This is entirely due to probabilistic features of the model. Specifically, random processes determine the exact number of houses which will turn vacant at each cycle and which purchasing power values will be selected from the purchasing power distribution at each cycle. Under these circumstances, even though the input parameters for two experiments may be identical, the output will not be. It follows, then, that the output values must be construed as estimates, and that observed differences between different experiments

Figures 3.8 and 3.9.   Another "Normal" Market

PROBABILITY OF LEAVING   .01
NUMBER SEEKING HOUSING   10
ACQUISITIVENESS*
PURCHASING POWER MEAN   17150.

* Acquisitiveness was set at 4 uniformly for all sellers during this experiment.

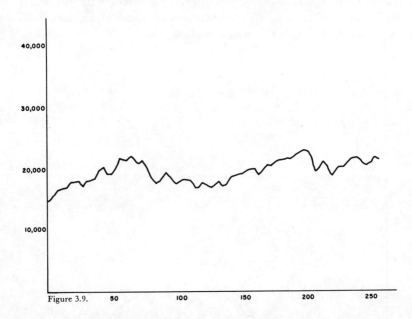

Figure 3.9.

are—in some measure—due to random variation. This can be seen by comparing Figures 3.8 and 3.9 with Figures 3.2 and 3.3. Both experiments have identical values of all input parameters, and both exhibit the same pattern of dynamic equilibrium at about the same level. They do differ, however, in detail.

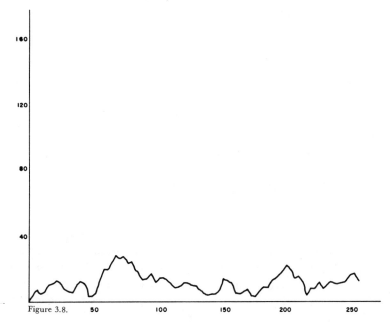

Figure 3.8.

This completes our discussion of the basic marketing model. Nowhere have we mentioned segregation or ethnicity. In the following chapters this omission will be remedied. We shall begin with an examination of the concept of segregation and proceed to a discussion of the model modified to permit the examination of ethnic factors.

4. The Nature of Segregation

One central concept in the study of ethnic residential patterns is segregation. Therefore, a good deal of attention in the present project was devoted to clarifying this concept. Two working papers were prepared, and a new measure of segregation was derived.[1] Since this measure is used in the present model, its development will be reviewed here.

4.1 Segregation: Intuitive Background

Segregation, like many concepts in sociology, has no universal meaning. Its meaning depends largely upon its user. For the most part, however, essayistic sociologists seem to be in agreement that residential segregation somehow refers to the degree to which members of a minority are all crowded in together in space.[2]

Liggitt, for example, talks of segregation when "people who are culturally or otherwise related to each other tend to live in separate areas within the urban community."[3] Similarly, Eldridge *et al.* describe as segregation the situation where "people or institutions of any one type are together in space."[4] And Green, in discussing race relations, considers segregation to be present when "categoric spatial separation" obtains between Negroes and whites.[5] Statements like these provide an intuitive basis for the term and suggest general rules for its use. Such statements, however, do not afford operational guides for the measurement of segregation.

Other writers have been concerned with measurement; they have devised operational indexes of segregation.[6] Such indexes are, of course, also definitions of the term. A problem arises, however, when the intuitive and operational definitions are compared: while the intuitive definitions all tend to stress spatial arrangements the operational indexes are uniformly based upon cumulative statistical distributions that are only indirectly concerned with space.

Duncan and Duncan have illuminated this problem.[7] They have shown that traditional segregation indexes have three features in common:

1. All are macro-measures; they are based upon the concentration of individuals in areal units. All, as a matter of fact, are functions of a single geometrical construct, the segregation curve.

2. This is true because all are designed to make use of existing census data. Data on the characteristics of individuals or households are not available for large populations. However, census tract or block summaries of a good many individual and household characteristics may be easily obtained from the U.S. Census.

3. As a consequence of this restriction to census data, all of the available measures represent serious compromises with the intuitive meaning of segregation.

These measures are all based upon the assumption that if each of a set of arbitrary spatial units (blocks, census tracts, or whatever) has the same proportion of a minority group, that group is not segregated. But if some units have too many, and others too few members of the minority, segregation is present. All the traditional measures, therefore, are based upon some index of the difference between the observed minority proportion in each unit and the assumed equality of proportion for all units. Thus, all stress consideration of the unevenness of the distribution of people of various types; none is sensitive to their spatial patterning. Space is taken into account only in the designation of blocks or census tracts as units of study. But the spatial location of persons within blocks or tracts is ignored as is the spatial location of the blocks or tracts with respect to one another. In short, traditional indexes of segregation are macro-measures. They are simple, inexpensive to calculate *but* they reflect only rather gross imbalances in the distributions of ethnic housing. In their neglect of spatial patterning they miss a major component of the intuitive meaning of segregation.[8]

In fact, at times the traditional measure may be seriously misleading. Figure 4.1, for example, shows a hypothetical city that is divided into four regular rectangular tracts. A minority is assumed to be confined to the shaded area in the center of the figure. The presence of such a minority ghetto suggests intuitively that a high degree of segregation is present. Standard segregation indexes, however, all agree that segregation in this city is absent.

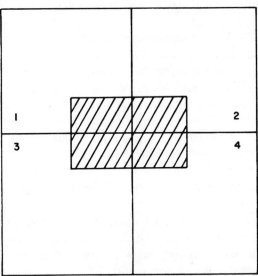

Figure 4.1.   A City with Four Tracks

Figure 4.2, on the other hand, shows another hypothetical city in which members of the minority are fairly well "spread out." In this case, however, tract lines are drawn (as they often are) in such a way that the minority is all included in a single irregularly shaped tract. Here the traditional measures would all show a high degree of segregation even though the minority seems to be distributed throughout the city.

Other examples might be given, but it is clear that to a great degree the standard measures do not reflect the sort of spatial

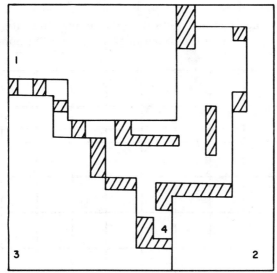

Figure 4.2.   A City with Four Tracks

patterning that is at the core of the intuitive concept.

According to Duncan and Duncan the traditional indexes are inadequate because they start with a limited set of (available) data and seek a mathematically convenient summary index.[9] What is needed, they say, is a rigorous theoretical system that will permit the development of a rationale for selecting and manipulating data.

It is this problem of developing an intuitively sound measure of segregation to which the present chapter is addressed. The proposed measure has a theoretical basis, though the economy of working with census data is sacrificed.

4.2   Segregation: A Measure

The unit of analysis in the present study is the household. Households are mapped to squares in the plane. All households are assumed to be arranged regularly with respect to their neighbors. That is, they have neighbors in even rows and columns. And the whole community to be studied is assumed to be rectangular in form. These ideas are pictured in Figure 4.3.

Concern will be centered upon the households occupied by some minority group, where minority status is defined as occupancy of less than half of the households in the community. Each household is assumed to be ethnically homogeneous—it is distinguishable as either minority (M) or non-minority, and that all households outside the community are considered non-minority.

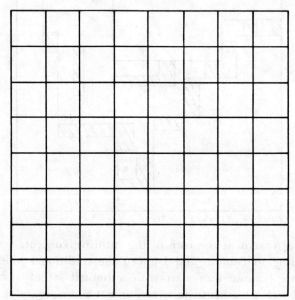

Figure 4.3.   The geometric model of a community where each square is one household

It was indicated above that, intuitively, segregation refers to the crowding together of members of a minority.   In present terms this suggests that segregation is a compact arrangement of M-squares in S.

According to Harris, "the word 'compact' means closely united or arranged so as to economize space."[10]   For areas of equal size, the most compact arrangement of objects is the one that permits the least exposure to other objects—the one with the shortest perimeter.   And the last compact arrangement is the one with the longest perimeter and therefore the greatest exposure.

The correspondence of this idea to segregation is clear.   Persons in a community may be considered to be segregated to the degree to which they are arranged compactly.   When the members of a minority group are, for example, all clustered into a single ghetto they are arranged compactly; they have relatively little exposure to the outside world, and they are segregated. If, on the other, hand, they are "spread out"—with non-minority group members between them—they are not compact. They have great exposure, and they are not segregated. For the present purpose, therefore, segregation will be defined in terms of compactness.

In order to examine the compactness of any set of M-squares the concepts of figure and perimeter are needed. The concept of figure is designed to allow for the examination of the spatial arrangement of minority households. A figure is an isolated minority household or a cluster of contiguous minority households bounded entirely by the non-minority community or by the external boundary of S. See Figure 4.4.

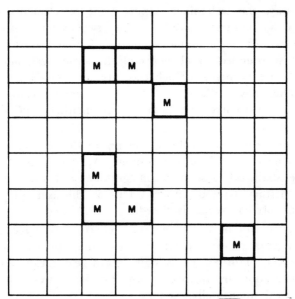

Figure 4.4. The community model showing four figures (with heavy outlines)

The perimeter (p), then is simply the length of the line enclosing the figures in S.

If, in general, minority households are surrounded by other minority households, p will be short, and the minority may be considered to be highly segregated.

By this same reasoning, we might define low segregation as the condition of maximum perimeter length. In this case minority households class would be systematically "spread out" over the available space. Each would, of course, then be surrounded by majority households.

Clearly, such an arrangement is not segregated. It is, however, still ordered, and one might suspect that the lack of segregation should be characterized by a lack of systematic order. If minority individuals were located at random—without reference to their minority status—segregation could not exist.

This phenomenon is expressed in the concept of "color blindness." If the individuals in a population were "color blind"—if they could not or would not distinguish between the minority and the non-minority—segregation would be impossible. In this case members of the minority would be *well-mixed* throughout the population.

In a way, the well-mixed arrangement of elements may be treated as a "half-way house" between two extreme ordered arrangements. At one extreme, elements of each class tend to be regularly surrounded by elements of the same class, and at the other extreme, elements of each class are surrounded by elements of the other class. Well-mixed sets of elements usually fall between these extremes—they occur when neither type of order predominates.

It would seem reasonable, therefore, to define segregation as one extreme of a bipolar continuum. At the other extreme is what we shall call systematic integration, and the zero point exhibits neither type of order. This is the conception upon which the present paper is based.

A measure will be developed that reflects the degree of order (either segregation or systematic integration) by its magnitude, and the type of order by its sign. Both segregation and systematic integration are defined as *ordered* departures from expectations based upon well-mixedness.

Segregation is that kind of order where minority households are crowded together. Hence, it yields a perimeter shorter than the expected value. Systematic integration, on the other hand, obtains when minority households are spread out. In a systematically integrated community the perimeter will be longer than its expected value.

Segregation may now be defined in terms of the length of the perimeter surrounding all the minority figures. For any number of minority households placed at random in a rectangular space the expected perimeter length is

$$E(P_n) = 4N_m - \frac{TN(N-1)}{S(S-1)}$$

where

T = the number of squares in the space that share a common side,

N = the number of M-squares,

and

S = the number of squares in the total space.[11]

Segregation is that kind of order where minority households are crowded together. Hence, it yields a perimeter shorter than the expected value. Systematic integration, on the other hand, obtains when minority households are spread out. In a systematically integrated community the perimeter will be longer than its expected value. If we take both of these considerations into account, we can define the following measure of both segregation and integration:

$$s_i = \frac{P_m - E(P_m)}{\left| P_{m\,Lim} - E(P_m) \right|}$$

where

P is the observed perimeter length,

E(P) = its expected length under the assumption of random arrangement of minority households,

and

P_{Lim} = the limit of P, either its minimum or its maximum.

The limit of **P** will, of course, depend upon the sign of

$$P - E(P).$$

If the sign is negative **P** is smaller than its expected value and

$$P_{Lim} = P_{Min},$$

the minimum value of **P**. It was proved that for an arbitrary number, **Q**,

$$P_{Min} = 4Q + 2 \text{ if } Q^2 + 1 \le N \le Q^2 + Q \text{ and}$$
$$4Q + 4 \text{ if } Q^2 + Q + 1 \le N \le (Q + 1)^2.$$

If the sign is positive, however,

$$P_{Lim} = P_{Max} = 4N$$

In this case s_i is a measure of integration.

In effect, we have defined two measures, one of segregation, one of integration. They are combined into a single index with the following properties:

(1) s_i is 0 if $\mathbf{P} = \mathrm{E}(\mathbf{P})$.   Therefore, if the minority households are well-mixed throughout the community s_i will be 0.

(2) s_i is $+$ if $\mathbf{P} > \mathrm{E}(\mathbf{P})$.   Thus, a positive value of s_i indicates integration, and the magnitude of s_i can be interpreted as a proportion of maximum integration.   If maximum systematic integration obtains $s_i = +1.0$.

(3) s_i is $-$ if $\mathbf{P} < \mathrm{E}(\mathbf{P})$.   A negative value of s_i shows segregation.   Again its magnitude can be interpreted as a proportion—this time as the proportion of maximum segregation.   With maximum segregation $s_i = -1.0$.

This index, s_i, is the measure of segregation used in the current model.   It is a micro-measure, sensitive to small variations in the locations of ethnic minority households, and it is related to the spatial arrangement of those households.

[1]L.C. Freeman, and J. Pilger, "Segregation: a micro-measure based upon compactness," Syracuse, New York: Systems Research Committee, Residential Segregation Study, Working Paper No. 1, 1964, and L.C. Freeman and J. Pilger, "Segregation: a micro-measure based upon well-mixedness," Syracuse, New York: Systems Research Committee, Residential Segregation Study, Working Paper No. 2, 1965.

[2]See, for example, P. I. Rose, *They and We*, New York; Random House, 1964.

[3]E. Liggitt, "The Urban Community," in *Introduction to Sociology* in Bossard, J.H.S., Lunden, W.A., Ballard, L.V., Foster, L., eds., Harrisburg, Pa.: Stackpole, 1952, p. 180.

[4]S. Eldridge, B. Berry, H.A. Gibbard, N.P. Gist, C.M. Rosenquist, and M.M. Willey, *Fundamentals of Sociology, A Situational Analysis*, New York: Thomas Y. Crowell Co., 1950, p. 204.

[5]A.W. Green, *Sociology, An Analysis of Life in Modern Society*, New York: McGraw-Hill, 1952, p. 325.

[6]W. Bell, "A probability model for the measurement of ecological segregation," Social Forces, 32 (1954), 357-364, W. Bell and E.M. Willis, "The segregation of Negroes in American cities: A comparative analysis," *Journal of Social and Economic Studies*, 6 (March, 1957), 59-75, D.D. Cowgill, "Trends in residential segregation of non-whites in American cities, 1940-1950," *American Sociological Review*, (February, 1956), 43-47, D.D. Cowgill and M.S. Cowgill, "An index of segregation based on block statistics," *American Sociological Review*, 16 (1951), 825-831, R.A. Hornseth, "A note on 'The measurement of ecological segregation' by Julius Jahn, Calvin F. Schmid, and Clarance Schrag," *American Sociological Review*, 12 (1947), 603-604, J.A. Jahn, "The measurement of ecological segregation: derivation of an index based on the criterion of reproducibility," *American Sociological Review*, 15 (1950), 100-104,

J.A. Jahn, C.F. Schmid, and C. Schrag, "Rejoinder to Dr. Hornseth's note on "The measurement of ecological segregation," *American Sociological Review* 13 (1948), 216-217, J.J. Williams, "Another commentary on the so-called segregation indices," *American Sociological Review,* 13 (1948), 298-303.

7O.D. Duncan and B. Duncan, "A methodological analysis of segregation indexes," *American Sociological Review,* 20, (1955), 210-217.

8In a recent article "Residential Segregation," *Scientific American,* 213 (1965), 12-15, Taeuber has proposed a new index. This index is, however, also subject to the restrictions described by the Duncans.

9O.D. Duncan and B. Duncan, *op. cit.*

10C.C. Harris, Jr., "A scientific method of districting," *Behavioral Science,* 9 (1964), 207-218.

11Proof of this and subsequent equations is given by L.C. Freeman, J.E. Pilger and W.E. Alexander, "Segregation: A Micro—Measure Based Upon Spatial Arrangements," forthcoming.

5. The Market with Ethnic Constraints

A general model of a housing market was introduced in Chapter 2. The axioms of that system, to the extent that they operate on the individual attribute of purchasing power, permit the development of neighborhoods segregated on a social class (or income) basis. Therefore, to the extent that different ethnic groups are characterized by differing class levels, that system will generate ethnic segregation. The income factor alone, however, is insufficient to account for observed patterns of ethnic residential segregation.[1] The concept of prejudice is needed. The object of this section, then, is to show how ethnic prejudice is used to modify the basic economic model. Here we shall use the Negro as the illustrative example of prejudice and discrimination, though without any loss of generality.

Explaining a prevailing state of residential segregation requires a systematic statement of the processes which eventuate in that condition. This calls for designating which variables are pertinent, specifying their interrelationships, and arranging these relational assertions to form a logically coherent system. The test of a theory, its ability to account for empirical data, rests not only on its logical elegance but also on the realism with which the original variables were selected and the adequacy of the relations postulated. It is at this point that empirical-descriptive materials

40

have an important bearing on theory-construction. In the materials that follow we have drawn upon the results of previous studies as much as possible. Where no data could be found we have tried to make reasonable estimates of the key parameters, variables and relations.

From a general overview of the empirical literature describing ethnic residential patterns, it appears that the segregation process is the output of the confluence of market-income facors, ethnic proximity-proportion factors, prejudice, and economic-interest factors. These factors control the level of residential segregation by (1) preventing non-whites from purchasing houses in white neighborhoods and by preventing them from remaining in such houses, and (2) by encouraging whites to move out of, or not to buy houses in, neighborhoods containing non-white residents.

In detail, the matter reduces to five questions. Can non-whites economically compete for houses in good quality white neighborhoods? Are brokers willing to bring homes in white neighborhoods to the attention of their non-white clients? Are white home owners willing to sell to prospective non-white buyers? Can a non-white who has successfully purchased a home in a white neighborhood actually live in his house? How likely is it that whites will move out and how likely is it that prospective white buyers will refuse to purchase a house in an ethnically or racially mixed neighborhood?

These are the questions that will be addressed in the present section. The answer to each, however, turns on prejudice in one way or another. We shall, therefore, begin with a discussion of prejudice.

5.1 Prejudice

Ethnic prejudice depends upon the existence of distinguishable ethnic groups. In the present model, two distinguishable groups are competing for housing: whites and Negroes. We present this distinction by defining two parameters:

(1)λ_w, the number of whites seeking housing per cycle, and

(2)λ_n, the number of Negroes seeking housing per cycle.

Each white person is assigned a prejudice score. Prejudice is

here conceived as a disposition, like acquisitiveness.[2] Prejudice
refers to a more or less stable consistency in the behavior of a
person over a range of acts with respect to a particular minority
group. Here it is assumed to be stable and to operate by either
increasing or reducing the probability that the person will per-
form a given act in a given setting.

Like acquisitiveness, prejudice, b, is here considered to be distributed in five ordered classes:

$$b = 0, 1, 2, 3 \text{ or } 4.$$

And its distribution form is determined by a single parameter,
δ, according to the schedule in Table 5.1.

As it is intended here, prejudice will be understood best in
terms of its use in the model. We shall, therefore, examine the
several equations that describe the constraints that are employed
in the ethnically sensitive market.

Table 5.1. Distribution of Prejudice.

δ Parameter	Probability of $b =$				
	0	1	2	3	4
0	1.0000	0	0	0	0
1	.8150	.1710	.0140	0	0
2	.2400	.4120	.2650	.0760	.0080
3	.0625	.2500	.3750	.2500	.0625
4	.2875	.1500	.1250	.1500	.2875
5	.0080	.0760	.2650	.4120	.2400
6	0	0	.0140	.1710	.8150
7	0	0	0	0	1.0000

5.2 The Economy and the Lender

It is clear from the outset that minority group members can—
and often do—differ from the majority in their economic condition. When it comes to buying a house, such differences are
likely to be exhibited in differential purchasing power, and,
therefore, in differential access to housing.

Purchasing power differentials may arise in two ways. First, there is no doubt that non-whites, and Negroes in particular, often occupy an inferior position in the economy. They are concentrated in low skill, low income, industrial and agricultural jobs. Therefore, they cannot compete effectively with whites across the broad spectrum of the housing market. This fact, also, has an important economic corollary. The economically inferior position of non-whites makes them comparatively poor credit risks from the viewpoint of managers of mortgage-money. This, of course, reduces their purchasing power further.

That is, however, not the end of the matter. The second basis for the potential economic disadvantage of non-whites results from discrimination in lending. Even if a Negro borrower is a good credit risk he may find that the lender will be unwilling to finance Negro house purchase in a predominantly white neighborhood. In part, this policy is self-serving: the lender, under the incorrect impression that Negro occupancy invariably depresses property values, wishes to protect its own investments in the area.[3] In part, it is a matter of "good" public relations, but whatever the rationalization, there is no doubt that lenders reinforce predispositions to residential segregation.[4]

It was necessary, therefore, to distinguish between two kinds of purchasing power in the present model: that for whites and that for Negroes. These may, of course, take the same values. In most realistic cases, however, we should expect the Negroes to have less purchasing power as a result of unequal opportunities in employment, discriminatory wages, and bias among lenders. The parameters for purchasing power, μ and σ, were, therefore, assigned separately for whites and Negroes. For whites they are μ_w and σ_w, and for Negroes, μ_n and σ_n. In this manner we can express any degree of inequality in purchasing power that is appropriate in a given application.

5.3 The Role of the Broker

Assuming that a Negro can afford to buy in a white neighborhood, his next task is to find a suitable house for sale. Here the real estate broker enters the picture.

It is almost always the case that the white broker will attempt to steer the non-white buyer away from houses in all-white neigh-borhoods. The techniques are well-known and the policy is often official—dictated by local real estate boards. These boards, by their ability to expel members and to mobilize business senti-ments against non-conformers, are able to exercise powerful restraints on trade. Beyond this, it appears that realtors, as indi-viduals, are sensitive to neighborhood feelings, and feel restrained from participating in the sale of a house to a non-white if, in their opinion, this would contravene neighborhood norms. Of course, once a neighborhood starts to undergo racial transition, brokerage biases are greatly reduced. Furthermore, it is reasonable to suppose that these biases might also be reduced in the face of an increasing proportion of houses on the market. A large num-ber of unsold houses suggests a low level of business activity. In such a case brokers would be inclined to be less sensitive to neighborhood feelings and more anxious to make a sale to any applicant regardless of his ethnicity.[5]

An attempt has been made to incorporate these relations into the present model. We can define a probability, f, that a Negro applicant will be shown a house. This probability depends upon three factors: (1) x, the proportion of Negroes in the neigh-borhood; (2) m, the mean level of prejudice in the neighbor-hood; and (3) u, the proportion of houses on the market in the neighborhood. The value taken by f in any particular circumstance is determined by a function expressing the assumed relationship between f and these other factors. For ease in communication, this function has been divided into five separate expressions. Together, these expressions define a unique value of f for each possible combination of values of x, m, and u.

In the first place, brokers are responsive to neighborhood pre-judice levels. In the extreme, when there is *no* prejudice in the neighborhood, there will be no restriction on the availability of houses for prospective Negro buyers regardless of the values taken by u and x:

Expression 5.1

$$f = 1 \text{ if } \begin{cases} m = 0 \\ 0 \le u \le 1 \\ 0 \le x \le 1. \end{cases}$$

This is a consequence of our basic definition of prejudice where a value of 0 indicates complete insensitivity to ethnicity.

Next, assuming that *some* prejudice is present, brokers will respond to the proportion of houses on the market in the neighborhood. They are, in effect, torn between the loss of income resulting from unsold houses on the market, and the fear of mobilizing neighborhood prejudice against themselves by selling to a Negro family. It is difficult to determine the conditions under which one or the other of these pressures will dominate. But intuitively, it would seem that as the proportion of houses on the market became large, immediate pressures to sell houses would take over. Under extreme conditions—when, let us say, over a third of the houses were on the market—it seems reasonable to assume that fears of long-range losses due to neighborhood reactions to Negro entry would be ignored in favor of immediate pressures to sell houses. Therefore, our second assumption is

Expression 5.2

$$f = 1 \text{ if } \begin{cases} 0 < m \leq 4 \\ u > .33 \\ 0 \leq x \leq 1. \end{cases}$$

When more than 33% of the houses are on the market, brokers will show houses to anyone regardless of race.

Brokers, will, of course, also respond to the proportion of Negro families established in a neighborhood in deciding whether or not to show a house to a Negro applicant. Depending upon neighborhood prejudice levels, the presence of some Negro residents will result in the area being defined as a "Negro neighborhood." And when the proportion of Negroes is above some point—regardless of prejudice levels—the neighborhood will be "opened up" to Negro residents.[6] For present purposes, we have assumed that this "opening up" phenomenon will occur when a neighborhood contains 10% or more Negro families:

Expression 5.3

$$f = 1 \text{ if } \begin{cases} 0 < m \leq 4 \\ 0 \leq u \leq .33 \\ x \geq .1. \end{cases}$$

If, at the other extreme, there are *no* Negro households in the neighborhood, the broker will be confronted directly with the potential conflict betwen his short and long range economic interest. As the proportion of houses on the market increases (up to the turnover point of 33%) he will feel pressure to sell. But to the degree that average prejudice is greater than 0, he will fear long range losses resulting from hostile reactions to his activities on behalf of Negro clients. Thus, his tendency to show available houses to Negro applicants will grow with either increases in vacancy rates or reductions in prejudice levels. In this case,

Expression 5.4

$$f = 1 - (1 - 3u)^{\frac{m}{4}} \quad \text{if} \begin{cases} 0 < m \le 4 \\ 0 \le u \le .33 \\ x = 0. \end{cases}$$

In this expression m and u work in opposite directions; f increases linearly with an increase in u and decreases linearly with an increase in m. As the proportion of vacancies approaches its maximum,

$$u \to .33,$$

the expression

$$1 - 3u \to 0,$$

and f is large. Conversely, as the average neighborhood prejudice level approaches its maximum,

$$m \to 4,$$

the expression

$$\frac{m}{4} \to 1,$$

and f is small. The numerical constants in this expression are used merely to establish the range for these linear relations.

Once Negroes have begun to enter the neighborhood (but are still less than 10%), however, the broker's conflict should disappear. Large proportions of vacant houses and high prejudice levels should work *together* to "open up" the neighborhood to entry of further Negro families. When prejudice levels are low, the presence of a few Negro households is not an occasion for concern. But in areas of high prejudice, even a small proportion of Negroes in the neighborhood leads to a white exodus. This, in turn, should increase the tendency of brokers to open the neighborhood to general Negro occupancy.

In this case, then, an increased proportion of houses on the market, high average prejudice levels, and an increased proportion of Negro households in the neighborhood should all work together to enhance the tendency of brokers to show houses to Negro applicants. Thus,

Expression 5.5

$$f = 1 - (1 - 3u)\left(1 - \frac{m}{4}\right)(1 - 10x) \text{ if } \begin{cases} 0 < m \leq 4 \\ 0 \leq u \leq .33 \\ 0 < x < .1. \end{cases}$$

These five expressions, 5.1 through 5.5, are the axioms that govern the behavior of real estate brokers in our model. They contain certain arbitrary elements, but the variables included and the relations between those variables expressed in the equations seem reasonable.

5.4 Refusal to Sell

The next big hurdle which the prospective non-white buyer must overcome is the white seller himself. Where the seller is a builder-developer and the neighborhood is new and suburban, the non-white is almost certain to be excluded.[7] Where the seller is a resident-owner the situation is slightly better. Here the prospective non-white buyer confronts the silent but powerful system of neighborhood white loyalties: the informal restrictive covenant. Custom and informal social sanctions, together with the belief that Negro occupancy injures property values, gives white owners sentimental and "rational" grounds for not selling to non-whites.[8]

However, this social conspiracy can be broken. Not every white property owner is prejudiced against non-whites or cares about his neighbors' good opinion. Furthermore, it may be in

the economic interest of a white owner to sell. Particularly if he
is highly acquisitive, a white seller will be unwilling to suffer the
economic deprivation entailed in keeping his house on the market
for an extended length of time while he waits for a white buyer.[9]
Here, as in the previous case we shall define a probability. In
this case we shall introduce s, the probability that a white
owner will be willing to accept an offer from a Negro buyer.
This probability is a function of four factors: (1) b, the prejudice
level of the owner; (2) z, the number of time cycles the house has
been on the market; (3) v, the acquisitiveness level of the owner;
and (4) x, the proportion of Negro households in the neighborhood.

The rationale for the owner's behavior parallels that for the
broker quite closely. First, as in the previous case, if the owner
is entirely without prejudice, he will sell without regard for the
ethnicity of the buyer:

Expression 5.6

$$s = 1 \text{ if } \begin{cases} b = 0 \\ 0 \leq z < \infty \\ 0 \leq v \leq 4 \\ 0 \leq x \leq 1. \end{cases}$$

To the degree the owner is unable to sell his house as time
passes, he suffers economic deprivation. In general, the impact of
such deprivation will depend upon his acquisitiveness level. There
is probably a point of deprivation, however, beyond which any
person, regardless of his prejudice or his acquisitiveness, is forced
to sell. In the present model we have assumed that this point
is reached after 25 time cycles. Then,

Expression 5.7

$$s = 1 \text{ if } \begin{cases} 0 < b \leq 4 \\ 0 \leq z \leq 25 \\ 0 \leq v \leq 4 \\ 0 \leq x \leq 1, \end{cases}$$

and an owner will sell to any interested buyer, regardless of race. An owner, like a broker is also assumed to be sensitive to the proportion of Negroes in the neighborhood. And again the reasoning runs that as more and more Negroes are present in the seller's neighborhood he will be less likely to resist selling his house because of ethnic bias. Finally, when the neighborhood contains 10% Negro occupants, we have proposed that, regardless of his prejudice level, the owner will sell to a Negro without question:

Expression 5.8

$$s = 1 \text{ if } \begin{cases} 0 < b \leq 4 \\ 0 \leq z < 25 \\ 0 \leq v \leq 4 \\ x \geq .1. \end{cases}$$

If, at the other extreme, the neighborhood contains no Negro families, the owner's probability of accepting an offer from a Negro buyer will be affected by the interaction of three factors: (1) the owner's prejudice level, (2) the length of time his house has been on the market, and (3) his level of acquisitiveness. High prejudice levels work to lower probability of sale to a Negro, while high acquisitiveness and a large number of time cycles on the market before sale raise that probability. Thus, if there are no Negro families established in the neighborhood,

Expression 5.9

$$s = 1 - (\frac{b}{4})(1 - \frac{z}{25})(1 - \frac{v}{4}) \text{ if } \begin{cases} 0 < b \leq 4 \\ 0 \leq z < 25 \\ 0 \leq v \leq 4 \\ x = 0. \end{cases}$$

Prejudice is again expected to have the opposite effect once Negroes enter the neighborhood. The highly prejudiced person is assumed to be anxious to get out in the face of Negro neighbors. Moreover, he is likely to fear a loss of property values resulting from Negro entry. Thus, rather than resisting sale to a Negro buyer, the prejudiced person will be eager to sell to a buyer of any type.

In this case, therefore, when
$$0 < x < .10,$$
delay in sale, acquisitiveness, prejudice and proportion of Negro households all work together to induce the seller to "give up" and sell to a Negro prospect:

Expression 5.10

$$s = 1 - (1 - \frac{b}{4})(1 - \frac{z}{25})(1 - \frac{v}{4})(1 - 10x) \text{ if } \left\{ \begin{array}{l} 0 < b \leq 4 \\ 0 \leq z < 25 \\ 0 \leq v \leq 4 \\ 0 < x < .1. \end{array} \right.$$

These five expressions, 5.6 through 5.10, are used to govern the behavior of sellers throughout the experiment.

5.5 Hostile Reactions

Once a Negro has purchased a house in an all-white neighborhood, he has still to take real possession of it, to live in it, and to enjoy its advantages. Newspaper stories describing the hazards experienced by non-white pioneers are all too common. Often there are subtle threats followed by an offer to buy his house by a newly formed local property owners association. If this does not work, physical violence may be employed.[10]

Too little is known about these pioneers and about the social conditions which control the level of threat which will be applied to them. It is probably the case that the average prejudice level of the neighborhood determines the lengths to which white residents will go to drive a Negro pioneer out. And it is probably true, that the longer the Negro remains, the greater will be the likelihood of his success in remaining in the neighborhood. In other words, whites have a certain "fatigue point" and movements toward fatigue are accelerated by the successful resistance of the first non-white entry. The appearance of additional non-whites has much the same effect.

These considerations have been incorporated into the model. We have defined r as the probability of a Negro family being "pushed out" of the neighborhood. The value taken by r depends upon m, the mean prejudice level, t, the number of other Negro households in the neighborhood, and k, the number of attempts already made to push this Negro family out.

This "pushing out" activity is assumed to obtain only for Negro residents who are new in the neighborhood. Thus, if an attempt is made to push a Negro family out for more than 3 cycles of time without success it is abandoned:

Expression 5.11

$$r = 0 \text{ if } \begin{cases} k \geq 3 \\ 0 \leq t \leq 239 \\ 0 \leq m \leq 4. \end{cases}$$

After 3 attempts, then, the probability of exit for a Negro household is exactly that for a white household, a.

Moreover, if there are three or more other Negro households established in the neighborhood, the extra push is stopped:

Expression 5.12

$$r = 0 \text{ if } \begin{cases} 0 \leq k < 3 \\ t \geq 3 \\ 0 \leq m \leq 4. \end{cases}$$

The first few Negro families, however, for the first few cycles of their residence, may be subjected to a push to get out, depending on the average prejudice level in the neighborhood. As time passes or if other Negro families are present, this push will be reduced. Thus,

Expression 5.13

$$r = (1 - \frac{t + k}{4}) \frac{m}{4} \text{ if } \begin{cases} 0 \leq k < 3 \\ 0 \leq t < 3 \\ 0 \leq m \leq 4. \end{cases}$$

Thus, both t and k reduce the effects of prejudice in mobilizing attempts to push Negro residents out of the neighborhood.

These expressions, 5.11, 5.12 and 5.13 are designed to express the effectiveness of the white community in its attempts to maintain its all-white character by pushing new Negro entrants back out.

5.6 The Ghetto Phenomenon

Naturally, if whites decide to move out of a neighborhood because of the presence of Negroes, and if such persons are not replaced by other whites, a new ghetto will be formed. In this matter, it appears that the decision to move out of a mixed neighborhood, or not to buy in one is, in part, conditioned by personal prejudice.

We have assumed that in making these decisions, prejudiced whites are not only responsive to the proportion of Negroes in the neighborhood, but also to their proximity as well.[11]

Proximity to and proportion of Negro neighbors are handled by defining a variable, h, the ethnic stimulus value of a house. For any given house the value of h depends upon the pattern of ethnic occupancy of surrounding houses.

The stimulus value of anything is its ability to elicit a response. By way of illustration, imagine a searchlight off in the distance. When the beam shines straight into your eyes the light has maximum stimulus value and as it moves to a point 180 degrees away its stimulus value declines. The stimulus value of the light (other things being equal) is contingent upon signal strength of the light and one's position relative to the axis of the beam.

Each house in a neighborhood, we assume, has a stimulus value for each other house. Events transpiring at one will be noticed by occupants of the others. But the importance of these events —their stimulus value—will depend upon distance and other spatial factors.

Distance d, as defined in the present study, is shown in Figure 5.1. Adjacent houses are at distance 1, houses across the street are distance 3, and so on. Associated with each distance is a saliency e. This is its potential ethnic stimulus value, so closer houses, of course, have much greater saliency. The relation used is

$$e = (6 - d)^2.$$

Thus, a next door neighbor has a saliency of 25, while that of a house in the next block is only 4.[12]

The ethnic stimulus value of a house, then, is simply the ratio of number of Negroes in the neighborhood—each weighted by the saliency of his location—the the maximum possible weighted number:

$$h = \frac{\displaystyle\sum_{d=1}^{5} a_d e_d}{432},$$

where:

a_d = the number of Negroes at distance d, and
e_d = the saliency of distance d.

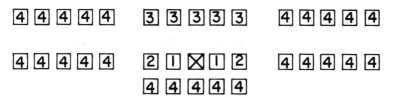

Figure 5.1. Distances of other houses from X. (All other houses in the neighborhood are at distance 5).

Our empirical knowledge of the influence of the proximity and proportion of Negroes on the decision of whites to leave the neighborhood is too weak to speak with real security about the process. There is a whole family of tangled contingent conditions: sentimental ties to the neighborhood which exercise inertial effects of white residents, their perceptual awareness of the density and proximity of non-whites, their estimates of the future of the neighborhood, the realistic alternatives available, and so on. Similar, though perhaps not identical, factors enter into the decision to buy into a mixed neighborhood.

Given the complexity of the situation, simplification for theoretical reasons is warranted, and in the present study we have assumed that the decision of whites to move out or buy a specific house in a mixed area is conditioned by immediate facts: personal prejudice levels and the ethnic stimulus value of the particular residence of concern.

This discussion shows the variables that come into play in the model. We have two simple functions that describe these relationships. First, o, the probability that a white owner will leave is

Expression 5.14

$$o = \begin{cases} 1 \text{ if } \dfrac{b}{4} - h > .5 \\[2ex] \dfrac{b\,h}{2} \text{ if } \dfrac{b}{4} - h \le .5. \end{cases}$$

Here, the degree of prejudice, b, of a white owner modifies his reaction to the ethnic stimulus value of his house. In the case of a potential white buyer, we determine p, the probability of his refusal to buy. It is

Expression 5.15

$$p = \begin{cases} 1 \text{ if } \dfrac{b}{4} - h > .25 \\[2ex] b\,h \text{ if } \dfrac{b}{4} - h \le .25. \end{cases}$$

Clearly the functions for o and p are similar. They differ only in that the expression for o contains a constant divisor, 2, and in that o and p have different threshold points,

$$\frac{b}{4} - h > .5 \text{ and } \frac{b}{4} - h > .25 \text{ respectively.}$$

If we compare these functions, the purpose of the differing numerical values becomes apparent. Selling out and not buying in a racially mixed neighborhood are similar acts; both are conditioned by prejudice. Yet it is "harder" to sell than not to buy. Given an identical ethnic stimulus value and identical prejudice level, it is here assumed that a prejudiced white is half as likely to sell as to refuse to buy. Moreover, the threshold for total refusal to buy comes twice as early as the threshold for total commitment to selling out. Thus, both selling out and refusal to buy are viewed as ordered along the same continuum. The exact numerical values of these constants is questionable, but the basic idea should be clear.

This, then, is the model for a neighborhood market with ethnic constraints. In the next chapter we shall see how it works.

[1]A.H. Pascal, *The Economics of Housing Discrimination*, Santa Monica, California: The Rand Corporation, 1965.

[2]For discussions of prejudice see G.W. Allport, *The Nature of Prejudice*, New York: Doubleday Anchor Books, 1954, M.L. De Fleur and F.R. Westie, "Verbal attitudes and overt acts," *American Sociological Review*, 23 (1958), 667-673, J. Greenbaum and L.I. Pearlin, "Vertical mobility and prejudice: a socio-psychological analysis," in Bendix, R. and Lipset, S.M. (eds.) *Class, Status, and Power: A Reader in Social Stratification*, Glencoe, Illinois: Free Press, 1953, A. Rose, *The Roots of Prejudice*, Paris: UNESCO, 1961, and R.M. Williams, Jr., *et al.*, *Strangers Next Door*, Englewood Cliffs, New Jersey: Prentice Hall, 1964.

[3]Adams, C., *Forbidden Neighbors*, New York: Harper and Brothers, 1955.

[4]Laurenti, L., *Property Values and Race: Studies in Seven Cities*, Berkeley and Los Angeles: University of California Press, 1959, and D. McEntire, *Residence and Race*, Berkeley and Los Angeles: University of California Press, 1960.

[5]McEntire, D., *op. cit.*, and R. Sterner, *The Negro's Share*, New York: Harper and Brothers, 1943.

[6]McEntire, D., *op. cit.*, and C. Rapkin and W. Grisby, *The Demand for Housing in Racially Mixed Areas*, Berkeley: University of California Press, 1960.

[7]McEntire, D., *op. cit.*

[8]Rapkin, C., and W. Grisby, *op. cit.*, R.C. Weaver, *op. cit.*, and A.M. Rose, "Inconsistencies in attitudes toward Negro housing," *Social Problems*, 8 (Spring, 1961), 286-292.

[9]Ball, H.V., and D.S. Yamamura, "Ethnic discrimination in the marketplace," *American Sociological Review*, 25 (October, 1960), 687-694, and N.A. Mercer, "Discrimination in rental housing: a study of resistance of landlords to non-white tenants," *Phylen*, 23 (Spring, 1962), 47-54.

[10]Handlin, O., *The Newcomers*, New York Metropolitan Regional Study, Cambridge: Harvard University Press, 1959, D. McEntire, *op. cit.*, C. Rapkin and W. Grisby, *op. cit.*, and G.E. Simpson, J.M. Yinger, *Racial and Cultural Minorities*, New York: Harper and Row, 1958.

[11]McEntire, D., *op. cit.*, C. Rapkin and W. Grisby, *op. cit.*, and A. Rose, *et al.*, "Neighborhood reaction to isolated negro residents, 2, an alternative to invasion and succession," *"American Sociological Review,* 18 (1953).

[12]The thinking underlying this conception is based upon the work of S.S. Stevens. See his paper, "A metric for the social consensus," *Science*, 151 (4 February, 1966), 530-541.

6. Simulation of the Market with Ethnic Constraints

In Chapter 3 above the output of a computer programmed to simulate a neighborhood housing market was discussed. Here the output of the complete model will be examined.

The introduction of ethnic prejudice complicates but does not contravene the economic principles expressed in the housing market. The same input parameters are entered, and the same output variables are recorded. But in the ethnically sensitive market, ethnic groups are distinguished (in this case white and Negro) and a distribution of ethnic prejudice is introduced. On the output side, we can count separately the whites and Negroes that enter the neighborhood, we can determine the proportion of houses that are occupied by Negroes, and we can measure the amount of segregation existing in the neighborhood at any time. The basic aim of this extended model, then, is to determine the effects of prejudice on the market economy and on the degree of residential segregation.

6.1 An Ideal: the Color-Blind Neighborhood

Let us imagine a neighborhood where we, as outside observers, can tell whites from Negroes, but the people involved cannot distinguish ethnicity. In a community of this sort prejudice would, by definition, be absent. Purchasing power, likewise, would be the same for both groups. Such a color-blind community is shown in Figures 6.1, 6.2, 6.3. Figure 6.1 shows the price at which houses sold, Figure 6.2 shows the number of houses on the market and Figure 6.3 shows the proportion of Negro families.

Figures 6.1, 6.2 and 6.3. A Color-Blind Neighborhood

PROBABILITY OF LEAVING	.01
NUMBER OF NEGROES SEEKING HOUSING	10
NUMBER OF WHITES SEEKING HOUSING	20
LEVEL OF ACQUISITIVENESS FOR BOTH	1
LEVEL OF PREJUDICE FOR WHITES	0
NEGRO PURCHASING POWER MEAN	14760.
WHITE PURCHASING POWER MEAN	14760.

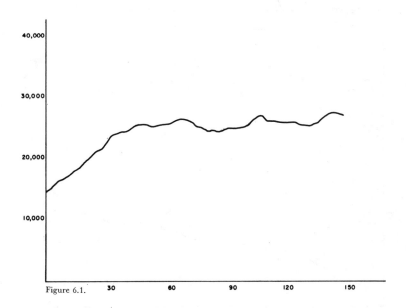

Figure 6.1.

If we consider the output of this simulation purely as a market we see essentially the same picture we saw in Chapter 3.[1] Demand is relatively high, and prices rise until they find their point of

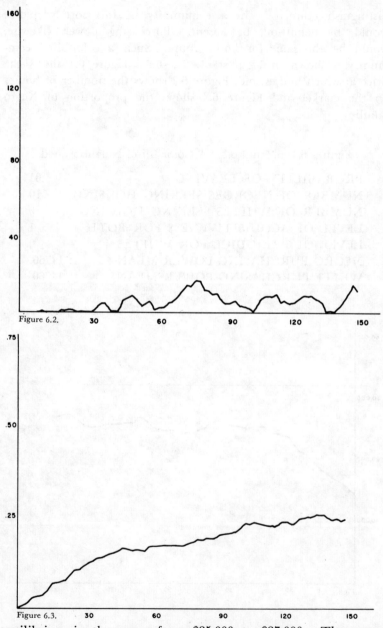

Figure 6.2.

Figure 6.3.

equilibrium in the range from $25,000 to $27,000. Thereupon they fluctuate around that average value. Vacancies vary as they did in the earlier experiment, and, economically speaking, this neighborhood turns out to be just about like those we examined earlier.

The ratio of Negroes to whites grows throughout the course of this experiment. Since Negroes and whites are indistinguishable, the proportion of Negroes in the neighborhood will grow until it approximates the proportion in the number seeking housing. In this case the Negroes will get their "fair share" of the market.

When the proportion of Negroes in the neighborhood is quite small the segregation ratio varies erratically. As the number increases, however, it settles down close to 0 as we should expect. A neighborhood containing 50 Negro families and yielding a segregation ratio of 0 is shown in Figure 6.4.

In summary, a color-blind community reveals the same dynamic market as that described in Chapter 3, and no segregation of Negroes.

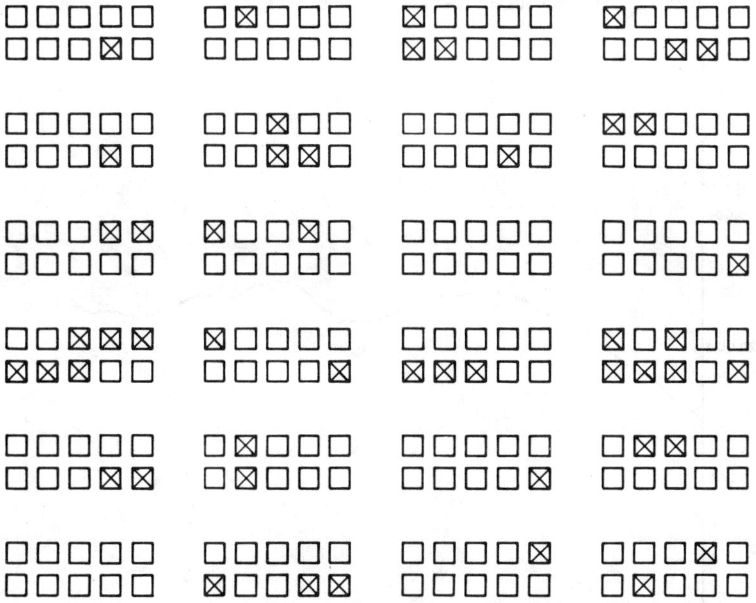

Figure 6.4. A Neighborhood without Segregation (Negroes are indicated by X; $s_i = 0.0$)

6.2 The Social Class Ghetto: Economically Based Segregation

The absence of prejudice with respect to housing is no guarantee that segregated housing will not develop. Consider the neighborhood described in Figures 6.5, 6.6 and 6.7. Again, prejudice with respect to housing is absent, but in this case economic discrimination is introduced. The purchasing power of whites averages $14,760, while that for Negroes is only $10,400. This might represent systematic discrimination on the part of employers or lenders. In any case, it has some consequences for the neighborhood.

Figures 6.5, 6.6 and 6.7.
An Economically Segregated Neighborhood

PROBABILITY OF LEAVING	.01
NUMBER OF NEGROES SEEKING HOUSING	10
NUMBER OF WHITES SEEKING HOUSING	20
LEVEL OF ACQUISITIVENESS FOR BOTH	1
LEVEL OF PREJUDICE FOR WHITES	0
NEGRO PURCHASING POWER MEAN	10400.
WHITE PURCHASING POWER MEAN	14760.

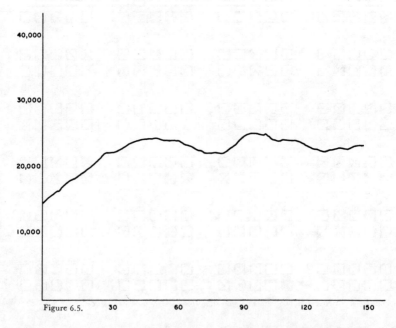

Figure 6.5.

The output reveals a market whose point of equilibrium is in the region of $23,000-$25,000. This is several thousand dollars below the market just discussed. The explanation, of course, lies in the decrement of demand occasioned by the reduction in the

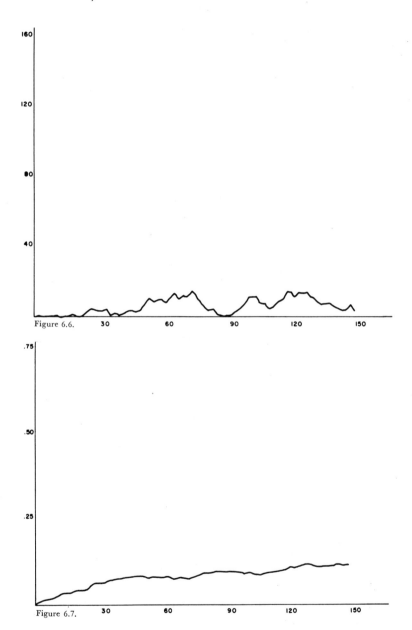

Figure 6.6.

Figure 6.7.

purchasing power of Negroes. This is confirmed by comparing the entries in the appendix for these two experiments. Fewer Negroes enter and higher vacancy rates obtain.

The values for the segregation index are small indicating that those Negroes who do enter the neighborhood are well-mixed. However, the proportion of all the houses in the neighborhood that are occupied by Negroes is reduced from .25 in the previous experiment to about .12 here. In short, economic discrimination, insofar as it eventuates in differentials in purchasing power, systematically excludes Negroes from certain segments of the housing market. The Negroes who can afford to live in this neighborhood are not segregated within the neighborhood, but the great bulk of Negro applicants are excluded entirely because of economic disadvantages. In a larger sense, then, we have a case of residential segregation without prejudice.

6.3 The Classical Case: Invasion and Succession

The neighborhood described in Figures 6.8, 6.9 and 6.10 is a classic case as reported in the literature on segregation. The distribution of prejudice is type 5; we have called this "southern moderate" but it is probably the distribution that has characterized most American urban communities for the past several decades. Only about 8% of the white population is assigned the lowest prejudice scores (0 and 1), while over 64% have high scores (3 and 4). Furthermore, economic discrimination is expressed in the differential between white and Negro purchasing power. In this neighborhood, then, we should observe the traditional symptoms of segregation as they have been described by sociologists.[2]

At the very outset it is clear that Negroes have a difficult time entering the neighborhood. For example, at Cycle 2 a Negro successfully bought a house but was forced out at Cycle 3. At the

Figures 6.8, 6.9 and 6.10. Invasion and Succession

PROBABILITY OF LEAVING	.01
NUMBER OF NEGROES SEEKING HOUSING	10
NUMBER OF WHITES SEEKING HOUSING	20
LEVEL OF ACQUISITIVENESS FOR BOTH	1
LEVEL OF PREJUDICE FOR WHITES	5
NEGRO PURCHASING POWER MEAN	10400
WHITE PURCHASING POWER MEAN	14760

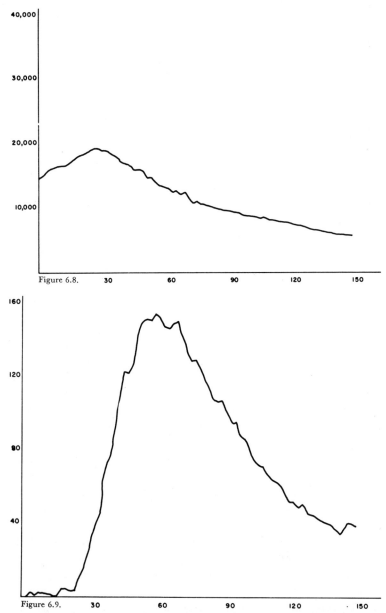

Figure 6.8.

Figure 6.9.

very same time, a second Negro moved in but he too was unable to consummate his purchase. It is not until Cycle 26 that Negroes become established in the neighborhood.

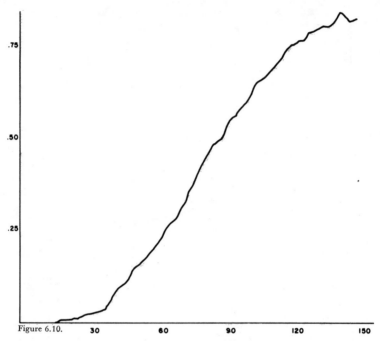

Figure 6.10.

This situation may be compared with the previous experiment which is like this in every respect but prejudice parameter level. Negroes, in that instance, immediately establish themselves in the neighborhood. The difference, of course, lies in the effect of prejudice in reducing the ability of the Negroes to see houses, to consummate sales with white sellers, and to remain in the neighborhood if they do buy houses. The effect is not simply the result of the prejudice levels of specific individuals; the principles of the model make Negro access to white neighborhoods dependent on the mean prejudice level of the neighborhood. In other words, it is the coupling of individual and collective traits that makes entry so difficult.

Once the penetration of the neighborhood is effected, however, it becomes progressively easier for Negroes to enter. Whites begin to leave, those with the highest prejudice levels and living closest to Negroes leaving first. And, although some whites continue to enter the community, prejudice exercises inhibitory effects so that demand cannot be maintained by new white purchasers. The upshot is that the vacancy rate builds up and prices turn downward.

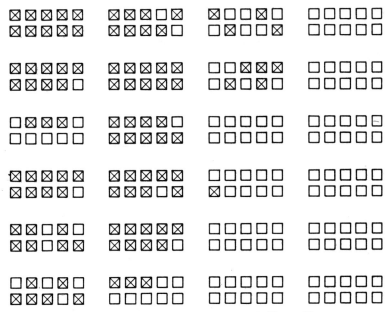

Figure 6.11.   A Segregated Neighborhood (Negroes are indicated by X; $s_i = .75$)

The process is cumulative and irreversible. The fall in prices brings the houses within the range of the Negro purchasing power distribution. Simultaneously, the fall in price increasingly inhibits whites from entering through the price-to-low-bid constraint. Then, as the proportion of Negroes builds up to rather large values, even relatively unprejudiced whites are unwilling to enter. The final result at Cycle 150 shows a neighborhood with 197 non-whites, 4 whites and 39 vacancies. This clearly is a case of invasion and succession. Furthermore, as one might expect, the segregation index achieves rather large values. (See Figure 6.11) Thus, segregation is maintained both within the neighborhood and in the larger community by the device of "turning this neighborhood over" to the Negroes. If equality in purchasing power had been allowed, the situation would be altered only in minor detail: at the end of the experiment the price level would have been about $6,980 instead of $5,750.

The fact that the process of population turnover in this neighborhood is not influenced much by purchasing power differentials, is itself an interesting fact about the model. What the model says is that in prejudiced communities, whites prefer whites to

Negroes as neighbors even though this pattern of preference eventuates in patterns of "social-class mixing." This follows from the inability of the ethnically prejudiced mentality—as given by the axioms of the model—to distinguish any variation in the minority group.

6.4 The Reservation: A South African Neighborhood Type

In South Africa, Negro-white relations are characterized by extreme prejudice levels. And strict segregation is maintained—even increased—by means of legislation. With extremely high prejudice levels, however, and consensus, apartheid type neighborhoods can be maintained even without legislation. Figures 6.12, 6.13 and 6.14 illustrate such a situation. Prejudice is at the maximum—uniformly 4 for all whites. Purchasing power is discriminatory, and white demand is enough to keep the prices up.

With these parametric settings no Negro even enters the neighborhood! This is indeed a white reservation. Strangely enough, however, in certain respects this neighborhood is similar to the one described in the color-blind neighborhood where there was absolutely no prejudice. The point of similarity is that in both instances, the market operates in economic terms; in both instances price levels are independent of prejudice.

What is happening is this: every time a Negro applicant appears in a neighborhood with an *extremely* high prejudice level, a series of operations is triggered to determine how many houses he shall be permitted to examine. If this is a non-zero value, the prospective buyer—as the reader will recall—is permitted to approach the sellers offering houses that fall into the set he can afford. Now, the extreme prejudice level short-circuits the ethnic aspects of the situation by rejecting Negro applicants regularly. In other words, the probability of both getting by the broker and actually consummating a sale is so fantastically small that for all practical purposes, the ethnic buyer does not even exist for this market. The consequence is that economic affairs in the matter of housing are entirely restricted to members of the white majority group. Prices, then, and vacancies are determined by white demand. In effect, the whites shut the Negroes out and run their own market.

Figures 6.12, 6.13, 6.14. A White Reservation

PROBABILITY OF LEAVING	.01
NUMBER OF NEGROES SEEKING HOUSING	10
NUMBER OF WHITES SEEKING HOUSING	20
LEVEL OF ACQUISITIVENESS FOR BOTH	1
LEVEL OF PREJUDICE FOR WHITES	7
NEGRO PURCHASING POWER MEAN	10400
WHITE PURCHASING POWER MEAN	14760

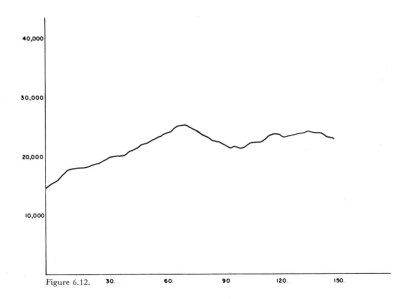

Figure 6.12.

The similarity between the reservation and the color-blind neighborhood is apparent. Prices rise, find a mean based upon supply and demand and vary around the mean. In the color-blind neighborhood the mean was in the range $25,000 to $27,000. Here, however, it is lower; it falls between $22,000 and $24,000. This is a consequence of the restricted demand that results from excluding Negroes from competing for houses. As a matter of fact, prejudice *always* reduces demand—either by excluding Negroes or through the refusal of whites to enter a mixed neighborhood—so there is always an economic cost to prejudice.[3]

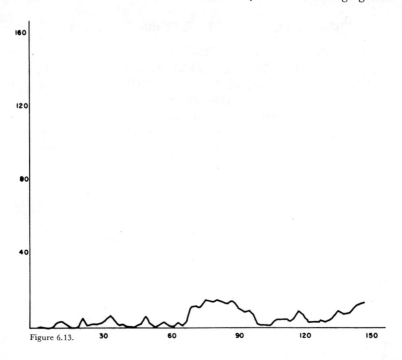

Figure 6.13.

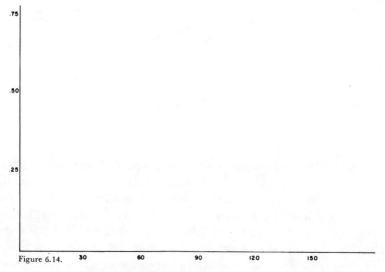

Figure 6.14.

These remarks specifically pertain to a situation where there are a sufficient number of white buyers to take up the vacancies and to prevent a serious decline in the price level. If it should develop what white demand is too small to do this, the model dictates that non-whites will ultimately enter. Essentially, here we are looking at the confluence of low white demand, and high acquisitiveness. As the number of unsold houses and the average length of time a house remains on the market both increase, the control of prejudice over economic activities diminishes. Once the first break occurs, the population of sellers is vulnerable to offers from Negroes, and the process rushes to its inexorable conclusion: a Negro reservation is created.

6.5 The Ethnically Mixed Neighborhood: A Possible Type

One of the problems that must be faced by any study of this kind is the prospect for a stable interethnic neighborhood. Many strategies might be tried. We might experiment with systematic location of Negroes or with restricting alternative locations for whites. But we suspected that under certain conditions of supply and demand, and given a rather moderate amount of prejudice, it would be possible for whites with relatively low levels of prejudice to generate enough demand to maintain an interethnic neighborhood. To do this we needed a rather large white demand, a moderate Negro demand, and a white population relatively low in prejudice. These characteristics were used to program the neighborhood shown in Figures 6.15, 6.16 and 6.17.

Figures 6.15, 6.16 and 6.17. An Interethnic Neighborhood, I

PROBABILITY OF LEAVING	.01
NUMBER OF NEGROES SEEKING HOUSING	10
NUMBER OF WHITES SEEKING HOUSING	20
LEVEL OF ACQUISITIVENESS FOR BOTH	1
LEVEL OF PREJUDICE FOR WHITES	2
NEGRO PURCHASING POWER MEAN	10400.
WHITE PURCHASING POWER MEAN	14760.

Negroes enter this neighborhood from the beginning. Some are pushed out, but most are there to stay. Those whites with the highest prejudice levels clear out and prices fall somewhat.

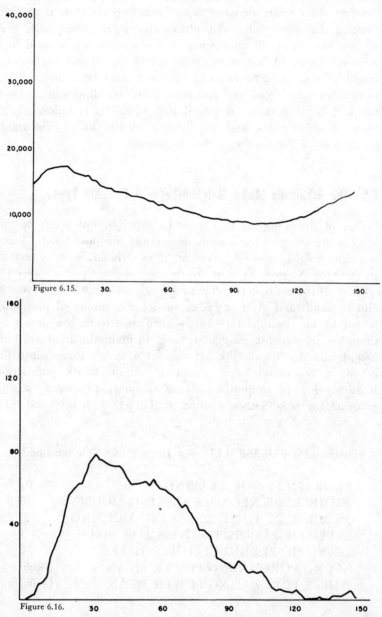

Figure 6.15.

Figure 6.16.

But white demand is high enough and prejudice low enough
that whites with relatively low prejudice levels do continue to
enter.   At one point more than 68% of the houses are Negro

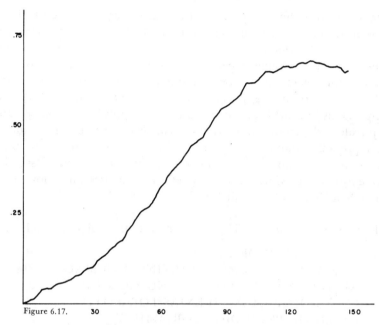

Figure 6.17.

occupied, but by the 150th Cycle that percentage has fallen to 65% we have, therefore, what looks like a stable interethnic neighborhood.

One sacrifice is involved in this process, however; the price levels drop to the $10,000 to $14,000 range. This is a consequence of reduction in demand because of selective white entry. Only those whites with relatively low prejudice levels enter. This economic loss can be reduced, however, by equalizing white and Negro purchasing power. This yields more Negro demand at higher price levels and results in the neighborhood shown in Figures 6.18, 6.19 and 6.20. Here, the final percentage of Negroes is in the same range, between 66% and 70%, and the final price is in the range of $18,000 to $22,000. Increasing white demand would, of course, result in even greater price levels and in a more socially desirable ratio of Negroes to whites. The key here is demand by unprejudiced whites; if it can be increased a better balanced interethnic neighborhood will result.

Note that in both of these neighborhoods the segregation level drops to zero. This is an additional consequence of the selective in-migration of unprejudiced whites.

A great many more experiments remain to be run on this

model neighborhood. Even at this early stage of investigation, however, certain general observations about this model can be made. It is evident that if Negroes cannot examine or buy houses with the same capability as white buyers, that this is—other things being equal—tantamount to a depression in demand. (Of course, from the perspective of the Negro applicant, this appears as an arbitrary constraint on supply.) Similarly, an equivalent depression in demand occurs whenever ethnic residential prejudice induces prospective white buyers to refuse to buy in a mixed neighborhood. Finally, prejudice influences supply by encouraging white owners to sell their houses and move out of a neighborhood once it has become mixed.

Figures 6.18, 6.19 and 6.20.   An Interethnic Neighborhood, II

PROBABILITY OF LEAVING	.01
NUMBER OF NEGROES SEEKING HOUSING	10
NUMBER OF WHITES SEEKING HOUSING	20
LEVEL OF ACQUISITIVENESS FOR BOTH	1
LEVEL OF PREJUDICE FOR WHITES	2
NEGRO PURCHASING POWER MEAN	14760.
WHITE PURCHASING POWER MEANS	14760.

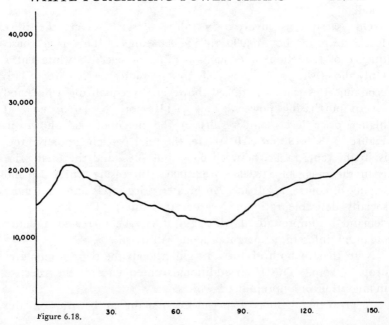

Figure 6.18.

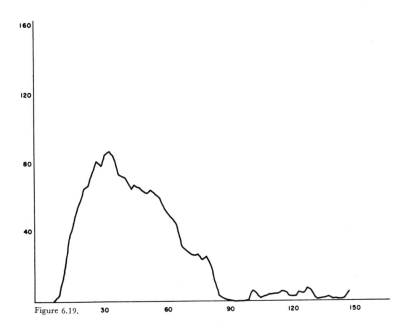

Figure 6.19.

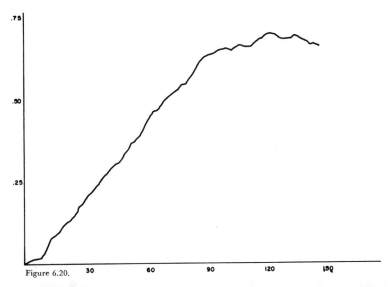

Figure 6.20.

In general, then, high prejudice levels lead to reduced house prices. This is true when prices under prejudice conditions are compared with prices in the no-prejudice situation. In practice, the entry of Negroes into even a highly prejudiced neighborhood will merely substitute Negro demand schedules for white demand schedules. If Negro demand is greater, prices will rise; if it is smaller, they will fall.

Finally, the present model shows that if white demand is high, Negro demand moderate, and prejudice not too extreme, stable interethnic neighborhoods are possible.

[1]Note that in this chapter acquisitiveness is distributed according to the parameter γ. In Chapter 3 a point distribution was used.

[2]Duncan, O.D., and B. Duncan, *The Negro Population of Chicago, A Study of Residential Succession,* Chicago: University of Chicago Press, 1957, and E.P. Wolf, "The invasion-succession sequence as a self-fulfilling prophecy," *Journal of Social Issues,* 13 (1957), 7-20.

[3]See A. Rose, *The Roots of Prejudice,* Paris: UNESCO, 1961, who shows the cost of segregated schools and other facilities.

7. In Conclusion: Some Comments on the Theory

This report has described the development of a preliminary theory and a computer model for ethnic residential segregation patterns. In the course of conducting this work we learned some things about our current model and can see ways in which it might be modified. Perhaps, the observations made in this chapter will be useful to other model-builders and to empirical investigators interested in segregation.

7.1 Findings and Implications for Policy

The present model, it must be admitted, has not been explored fully. Computer simulation is an efficient technique for experimentation. In the words of Markowitz and Karr it

". . . pre-tests proposals under alternate contingencies in advance of implementation. To a certain extent it provides hindsight in advance."[1]

Only a few experiments, however, have so far been conducted. Nevertheless, in spite of the small sample of input combinations that have been tried, certain features stand out.

The first thing that comes to mind, is the delicate character of the ethnic residential segregation system. Specifically, experiments thus far conducted with this model, indicated that under most conditions neighborhoods have strong predispositions to go to extremes: the white (host) population resists Negro invasion with great success or it abandons the neighborhood. Of course, our experiments show that, under conditions of low prejudice, it is possible to establish and maintain an ethnically mixed neighborhood, but even there the proportion of Negroes is too high. The point is that even a small departure from the optimum condition of no prejudice results in a socially unacceptable ratio of Negroes to whites and therefore in an appreciable degree of segregation.

There is, however, another consequence of the responsiveness of this system to levels of prejudice. Experiments with the model show that Negroes cannot break into neighborhoods characterized by extreme prejudice. In that case, the distribution of prejudice is a point distribution: every white resident has the maximum prejudice score. If it is assumed that this is unlikely, that there will always be a few relatively unprejudiced persons living in a neighborhood, then we can show by means of other experiments, that, given Negro demand, the likelihood of maintaining a completely white neighborhood is small. Again, minor adjustments in initial conditions can result in sizeable social changes.

The second thing that our experiments make clear is that there is no simple relationship between Negro "invasion" of a neighborhood and house prices. In the model—and probably in actual communities—house price is simply a function of supply and demand. If a neighborhood housing market is restricted to whites, house prices will be determined by exit probability and the number of whites seeking housing. Now if Negroes appear on the scene, and the whites are unprejudiced, the result is simply an increase in demand because of the additional persons seeking housing.

If, on the other hand, the whites are highly prejudiced and Negroes succeed in entering the neighborhood, it will simply be turned over to them. In this case white demand is replaced by Negro demand. If Negro demand is greater, prices will rise, if it is smaller, they will fall.

A moderate prejudice distribution will tend to exclude some whites from competition for housing in a mixed neighborhood. The point of price stabilization in this case depends upon the remaining demand—of Negroes and unprejudiced whites—after the prejudiced whites are excluded. In any case, the results of these experiments corroborate those of Laurenti who asserts that when Negroes enter a neighborhood prices may rise or fall or remain stable.[2]

A third general finding involves the economic cost of prejudice. When whites are prejudiced, either Negroes are excluded, or—if they enter—other whites will not. In either case demand is diminished and prices fall. When Negroes are numerically in the minority, therefore, it may be to their economic advantage to maintain a certain amount of white prejudice. In that way they can compete only with other Negroes, in a Negro economy, and enjoy the same housing for less money.

Clearly, this situation is socially undesirable. Furthermore, even the economic advantage is probably only relative. Inasmuch as high prejudice levels are invariably associated with strong economic discrimination, these Negroes would still pay relatively more of their income for housing than would corresponding whites.[3] The loss to the total economy, however, is clear.

In the matter of policy implications the model confirms some obvious things and suggests some not-so-obvious things. We shall deal with the latter.

First, we note that equality of purchasing power alone does not prevent a condition of intra-neighborhood segregation; in the face of local prejudice such equality merely speeds up the process of population turnover. If there is no residential prejudice, and ethnic inequality in purchasing power exists, there will still be segregation, this time by the systematic exclusion of Negroes from "better" neighborhoods. It follows, then, that equal access to decent neighborhood and housing conditions requires equality across the board.

It might be argued that population turnover occurs because there is too much non-white demand; consequently, purchasing power differentials are, in a sense, desirable. All one can say to that argument is that (1) when prejudice exists, income differentials merely postpone the process to the point where falling prices come within the range of the ethnic buying power distribution, and (2) if prejudice and income differentials exist simultaneously, the fall in prices will be accentuated even more.

Second, the model indicates density and spatial distribution factors should be related in an ameliorative policy. Specifically, if prejudice obtains and the non-white population is segregated in a certain area of a neighborhood, houses on the perimeter of the non-white area are offered for sale. Since these will be filled by newly entering whites only with difficulty, they are likely to be sold to Negroes. This wave process culminates in a more or less complete turnover of the population. On the other hand, if the same initial number of non-whites could be dispersed, the turnover process would be slowed. This has not been demonstrated experimentally so far, but it appears to be a reasonable conclusion.

Third, there is a class of "administrative" solutions implied by the model. Negro demand could be cut off at a certain point, and in conjunction with this, white demand could be maintained —if need be—by subsidies. Perhaps, it would be possible to arrange the addresses of incoming white applicants judiciously so that the distance of a prejudiced white from the closest Negro is proportional to his prejudice level.

Naturally, it is hard to see how these principles could be invoked without weakening the doctrine of consumer sovereignty. There is some reason to suspect, however, that if Negro demand can be kept fairly low and white demand high, that unprejudiced whites would tend to form a "buffer zone" between Negroes and prejudiced whites. This might well result from a "natural" process, and require only the manipulation of demand through the control of alternatives. This, and other related hypotheses will be examined in future work with the housing model.

7.2 Some Need Revisions

The model of a neighborhood housing market presented in this report needs to be modified in order to make it more realistic and serviceable as the basis for a theory of ethnic residential segregation patterns. Some of these modifications can only be made as a consequence of empirical study, others can be made prior to research.

In the first case, one point of concern is in the nature of the relations expressed in the equations governing each phase of the market process. Specifically, the equations governing brokerage behavior, are premised on the assumption of linearity. These equations deal with the relations among several variables; invariably, those relations are expressed in linear form.

Linearity, of course, has the virtue of simplicity, and in the initial stages of theory-construction it is legitimate to resort to such stratagems. However, it cannot be supposed with impunity that nature conforms to such simple and elegant rules. Only empirical research can dictate how these postulated relations should be modified.

There are a variety of other places where the realism of the model undoubtedly suffers from gaps in empirical research. Much more information about the nature of our experimental input parameters is required. For example, we would like to know how financial acquisitiveness and prejudice are actually distributed in a population of homeowners and prospective buyers. We would also like to know more about individual economic decision-making in the area of buying and selling houses: specifically, how individuals modify their selling price in the event of not selling, and how buyers determine their lower price limits.

The empirical research that is needed to improve the realism of the model will not always be easy. In fact, there are certain places in the model which are exceptionally challenging. For example, "acquisitiveness" has been deployed in the model as an hypothetical construct. We believe that this is a meaningful concept, but we do not know—in a technical sense—its empirical manifestations, its distributions, and its relation to other social-psychological traits.

Another place in the model that will require a good deal of work is the influence of ethnic proportion-distribution factors on the decision of a white person to move out or to refuse to buy a given house. The model determines the social stimulus value of Negroes in other houses. Houses on the same side of the street as the house of reference and immediately adjacent to it are coded at distance "1," while houses across the street are coded distance "3." These numerical values, when entered into the formula, operate so that five Negroes across the street have about the same stimulus value for a white occupant as two Negro immediate neighbors. Now, it seems perfectly safe to distinguish—as the model does—between the Negro resident next door and the one across the street, but we do not know whether the units established are empirically sensible.

Then too, empirical research is required to permit us to establish a correspondence between computer time cycles and real time. Lacking such information, it is never really clear whether or not a process is rushing or dawdling along.

There are other ways the model might be modified to make it more realistic and sophisticated and these changes can be made in the absence of factual information. For example, in the current model, if a house is not sold, its selling price is regularly decremented. It is possible, therefore, that the price of a house might be completely unrelated to the current market. Admittedly, this is unreasonable, but it is a small problem.

Of greater significance are changes designed to increase the sophistication of the model—changes that are designed to improve the fit of the general model to the complexities of the external world. First, it should be noted that the experimental neighborhood is isolated from other neighborhood housing markets and from long run social changes. It is seldom the case that the person who buys a house in a given neighborhood does so because he has no alternatives. Ordinarily, a fairly competitive situation prevails, with new housing competing with old, and one neighborhood competing with another. In a way, the prevailing vacancy rate and the number seeking housing are indicative of the competitive power of that area vis-a-vis other areas. But explicit concern with such factors is limited in the current model.

A solution lies in expanding the domain of concern by treating three or more neighborhoods. In that case, the minimal requisites for the study of segregation as a form of selective migration would exist: each person would have a current location, a past location, and a future location. In addition to this, the use of several neighborhoods would permit more elaborate experiments in the area of social choice and rationality. For example, under the present model, people move out for one reason or another, but this set of reasons should include, in a formal way, the probability of finding an equivalent or superior house.

Also, in the current model, there is no relation between prejudice level and ethnic purchasing power differential. As it stands now, white-Negro purchasing power differential is an independent variable. It is reasonable, however, to assume that this differential is dependent upon prejudice; in that case, the model might be improved by rearranging it so that the income differential is directly proportional to the level of prejudice that prevails.   Under these conditions we could simulate the ideological traits of the larger society.   Still, it would be necessary to take into account the losses involved in such a situation.   If purchasing power is under direct experimental control it is possible to examine the separate effects of the purchasing power variable and the prejudice variable.   In other words, the alteration would make it difficult to explore the social class and ethnicity components in the residential segregation process.

The model is static in certain ways.   Specifically, individuals are assigned a prejudice score and this score does not change over the course of an experiment.   Prejudice level, of course, is not a fixed attribute; it may be modified by experience. Our model does not take this into account.

Finally, a more sophisticated model would attend more closely to interpersonal sociological aspects of community life.   Under the current model the only critical "social facts" at work are the atmosphere of prejudice (the mean prejudice level) as it affects attempts to force new Negro buyers out.   It would be highly desirable to extend the model so that it is capable of dealing with contagion processes such as those that encourage flight, adaptation, and resistance.

Research along all of these lines would improve the model greatly.   We believe the model is worthy of this additional work.

This, then, is our theory as it stands currently.   It is far from finished, but it is a step toward organizing knowledge in the area of ethnic segregation.   Hopefully it may be useful in guiding the collection of data and in suggesting some ways of thinking about segregation.[4]

[1]Markowitz, H., and H.W. Karr, "Simulation modeling and programming by means of the Simscript simulation programming language," brochure of the California Analysis Center, Inc., n.d.

[2]Laurenti, L., *Property Values and Race: Studies in Seven Cities*, Berkeley and Los Angeles: University of California Press, 1959.

3Dollard, J., *Caste and Class in a Southern Town,* New Haven: Yale University Press. 1937.

4An extremely suggestive alternative approach has been proposed by R.L. Morrill, "How ghettoes grow: problems and alternatives," University of Washington, mimeograph, n.d.

Glossary of Symbols

Parameters

α = probability of a house placed on the market.

γ = distribution form for acquisitiveness.

δ = distribution form for prejudice.

λ_w = number of whites seeking housing per cycle.

λ_n = number of Negroes seeking housing per cycle.

λ = number seeking housing when ethnicity is irrelevant.

μ_w = mean of the normal distribution underlying the lognormal distribution of purchasing power by Whites.

μ_n = mean of the normal distribution underlying the lognormal distribution of purchasing power for Negroes.

μ = mean of the normal distribution underlying the lognormal distribution of purchasing power when ethnicity is irrelevant.

σ_w = standard deviation of the normal distribution underlying the lognormal distribution of purchasing power for whites.

σ_n = standard deviation of the normal distribution underlying the lognormal distribution of purchasing power for Negroes.

σ = standard deviation of the normal distribution underlying the lognormal distribution of purchasing power when ethnicity is irrelevant.

83

Variables

a_d = number of Negroes at distance d.

b = prejudice score.

d = distance from a house of reference to another specified house.

e_d = saliency of a house at distance d.

f = probability of a Negro applicant being shown an available house.

h = ethnic stimulus value of a Negro-occupied house with respect to a house of reference.

k = number of attempts made to push out a Negro resident.

m = mean prejudice level in the neighborhood.

n = asking price for a house on the market.

o = probability that a white owner will place his house on the market.

p = probability that a white prospect will refuse to buy a house.

r = probability that a Negro resident will be pushed out of a house.

s_i = segregation-integration level of neighborhood.

t = number of Negro households in the neighborhood minus 1.

u = proportion of houses on the market.

v = acquisitiveness score.

w = purchasing power in dollars.

x = proportion of Negroes in the neighborhood.

y = pricing average.

z = number of cycles a house is on the market.

Bibliography

Abrams, C. *Forbidden Neighbors,* New York: Harper and Brothers, 1955.

Aitchison, J. and Brown, J. A. C. *The Lognormal Distribution,* Cambridge: Cambridge University Press, 1957.

Allport, G. W. *The Nature of Prejudice,* New York: Doubleday Anchor Books, 1954.

Ball, H. V. and Yamamura, D. S. "Ethnic discrimination in the marketplace," *American Sociological Review,* 25 (October, 1960), 687-694.

Bell, W. "A probability model for the measurement of ecological segregation," *Social Forces,* 32 (1954), 357-364.

Bell, W. and Willis, E. M. "The segregation of Negroes in American cities: a comparative analysis," *Journal of Social and Economic Studies,* 6 (March, 1957), 59-75.

Berelson, B. and Steiner, G. A. *Human Behavior: An Inventory of Scientific Findings,* New York: Harcourt, Brace and World, 1964.

Braithwaite, R. B. *Scientific Explanation,* New York: Harper and Brothers (Harper Torchbooks), 1960.

Coleman, J. S. *Introduction to Mathematical Sociology,* Glencoe, Illinois: Free Press, 1964.

Cowgill, D. D. "Trends in residential segregation of non-whites in American cities, 1940-1950," *American Sociological Review,* (February, 1956), 43-47.

Cowgill, D. O. and Cowgill, M. S. "An index of segregation based on block statistics," *American Sociological Review,* 16 (1951), 825-831.

De Fleur, M. L. and Westie, F. R. "Verbal attitudes and overt acts," *American Sociological Review,* 23 (1958), 667-673.

de Sola Pool, I. "Simulating social systems," *International Science and Technology* (March 1964), 62-70.

Dollard, J. *Caste and Class in a Southern Town,* New Haven: Yale University Press, 1937.

Duncan, O. D. and Duncan, B. "A methodological analysis of segregation indexes," *American Sociological Review*, 20 (1955), 210-217.

Duncan, O. D. and Duncan, B. *The Negro Population of Chicago, A Study of Residential Succession*, Chicago: University of Chicago Press, 1967.

Freeman, L. C. and Pilger, J. "Segregation: a micro-measure based upon compactness," Syracuse, New York: Systems Research Committee, Residential Segregation Study, Working Paper No. 1, 1964.

Freeman, L. C. and Pilger, J. "Segregation: a micro-measure based upon well-mixedness," Syracuse, New York: Systems Research Committee, Residential Segregation Study, Working Paper No. 2, 1965.

Glazer, N. and McEntire, D. (eds.) *Studies in Housing and Minority Groups*, Berkeley: University of California Press, 1960.

Greenblum, J. and Pearlin, L. I. "Vertical mobility and prejudice: a socio-psychological analysis," in Bendix, R. and Lipset, S. M. (eds.) *Class, Status, and Power: A Reader in Social Stratification*, Glencoe, Illinois: Free Press, 1953.

Handlin, O. *The Newcomers*, New York Metropolitan Regional Study, Cambridge: Harvard University Press, 1959.

Harris, C. C., Jr. "A scientific method of districting," *Behavioral Science*, 9 (1964), 207-218.

Hornseth, R. A. "A note on 'The measurement of ecological segregation' by Julius Jahn, Calvin F. Schmid, and Clarence Schrag," *American Sociological Review*, 12 (1947), 603-604.

Jahn, J. A. "The measurement of ecological segregation: derivation of an index based on the criterion of reproducibility," *American Sociological Review*, 15 (1950), 100-104.

Jahn, J. A., Schmid, C. F. and Schrag, C. "Rejoinder to Dr. Hornseth's note on the 'The measurement of ecological segregation,' " *American Sociological Review*, 13 (1948), 216-217.

Jahn, J. A., Schmid, C. F. and Schrag, C. "The measurement of ecological segregation," *American Sociological Review*, 12 (1947), 293-303.

Laurenti, L., *Property Values and Race: Studies in Seven Cities*, Berkeley and Los Angeles: University of California Press, 1959.

Markowitz, H. and Karr, H. W. "Simulation modeling and programming by means of the Simscript simulation programming language," brochure of the California Analysis Center, Inc., n.d.

McClelland, D. C., *The Achieving Society*, Princeton, New Jersey: Van Nostrand, 1961.

McEntire, D. *Residence and Race*, Berkeley and Los Angeles: University of California Press, 1960.

McGinnis, R. *Mathematical Foundations for Social Analysis*, Indianapolis: Bobbs-Merrill, 1965.

Mercer, N. A. "Discrimination in rental housing: a study of resistance of landlords to non-white tenants," *Phylen*, 23 (Spring, 1962), 47-54.

Miller, E. W. *The Negro in America: A Bibliography*, Cambridge, Massachusetts: Harvard University Press, 1966.

Moran, P. A. "The interpretation of statistical maps," *Journal of the Royal Statistical Society*, B, 10 (1948), 243-251.

Morrill, R. L. "How ghettoes grow: problems and alternatives," University of Washington, Mimeograph, n.d.

Murray, H. A. (ed.) *Explorations in Personality*, New York: Oxford University Press, 1938.

Pascal, A. H. *The Economics of Housing Discrimination*, Santa Monica, California: The Rand Corporation, 1965.

Rapkin, C. and Grisby, W. *The Demand for Housing in Racially Mixed Areas*, Berkeley: University of California Press, 1960.

Rapkin, C., Winnick, L. and Blank, D. M. *Housing Market Analysis, A Study of Theory and Methods*, Washington: U. S. Government Printing Office.

Richardson, L. F. "The problem of contiguity: an appendix to 'Statistics of Deadly Quarrels,'" *General Systems*, 6 (1961), 139-187.

Rose, A., "Inconsistencies in attitudes towards Negro housing," *Social Problems*, 8 (Spring, 1961), 286-292.

Rose, A. *The Roots of Prejudice*, Paris: UNESCO, 1961.

Rose, A., *et al.* "Neighborhood reaction to isolated Negro residents, 2, an alternative to invasion and succession," *American Sociological Review*, 18 (1953).

Rose, P. I. *They and We*, New York: Random House, 1964.

Rossi, P. H. *Why People Move*, Glencoe, Illinois: Free Press, 1955.

Samuelson, P. A. *Economics, An Introductory Analysis*, New York: McGraw-Hill, 1948.

Samuelson, P. A. "A note on measurement of utility," *Review of Economic Studies*, 4 (1937), 155-161.

Schelling, T. C. "An essay on bargaining," *American Economic Review*, 46 (1965), 281-306.

Simpson, G. B. and Yinger, J. M. *Racial and Cultural Minorities*, New York: Harper and Row, 1958.

Sterner, R. *The Negro's Share*, New York: Harper and Brothers, 1943.

Stevens, S. S. "A metric for the social consensus," *Science*, 151 (4 February, 1966), 530-541.

Vickrey, W. "Measuring marginal utility by reactions to risk," *Econometrica*, 13 (1945), 319-333.

Weaver, R. C. *The Negro Ghetto*, New York: Harcourt, Brace, 1948.

Williams, J. J. "Another commentary on the so-called segregation indices," *American Sociological Review*, 13 (1948), 298-303.

Williams, R. M., Jr., *et al. Strangers Next Door*, Englewood Cliffs, New Jersey: Prentice Hall, 1964.

Wolf, E. P. "The invasion-succession sequence as a self-fulfilling prophecy," *Journal of Social Issues*, 13 (1957), 7-20.

Computer Output

Table 1. Simulated "Normal" Market

PROBABILITY OF LEAVING	.01.
NUMBER SEEKING HOUSING	10
ACQUISITIVENESS*	
PURCHASING POWER MEAN	17150.

---

*Acquisitiveness was set at 4 uniformly for all sellers during this experiment.

CYCLE NUMBER	EXIT RATE	ENTR RATE	TOTAL VACANT	AVERG COST	PRIC AVERG
					15000.
1	4	1	3	16500.	15150.
2	4	1	6	16660.	15310.
3	2	1	7	16840.	15500.
4	2	2	7	16520.	15800.
5	6	5	8	16310.	16460.
6	1	3	6	16310.	16350.
7	0	1	5	17730.	16420.
8	0	3	2	16340.	16440.
9	0	1	1	14000.	16270.
10	5	2	4	15810.	16130.
11	3	0	7	0.	16130.
12	2	3	6	17620.	16520.
13	4	1	9	18170.	16560.
14	2	1	10	18220.	16750.
15	4	1	13	18430.	16960.
16	1	4	10	18060.	17990.
17	1	3	8	16380.	17620.
18	0	1	7	19390.	17740.
19	1	1	7	16980.	17620.
20	3	4	6	18470.	17690.
21	1	3	4	17540.	17960.
22	4	1	7	13990.	17680.
23	4	2	9	13710.	16790.
24	2	1	10	18470.	16700.
25	4	2	12	15910.	16000.
26	2	1	13	18290.	16260.
27	8	1	20	17920.	16100.
28	0	1	19	17280.	15960.
29	4	3	20	17560.	17010.
30	2	1	21	18710.	17510.
31	1	3	19	17540.	17750.
32	4	2	21	17050.	17530.
33	0	3	18	18010.	17700.
34	3	4	17	18470.	17890.
35	3	1	19	15180.	17720.
36	2	3	18	17440.	17630.
37	4	3	19	17090.	17320.
38	3	2	20	16660.	16760.
39	1	7	14	15290.	15940.
40	2	5	11	17190.	16510.

41	2	2	11	18160.	16880.
42	2	3	10	14830.	16680.
43	3	5	8	14560.	15360.
44	4	2	10	17890.	15300.
45	2	1	11	17610.	15770.
46	0	2	9	16490.	15910.
47	1	3	7	16190.	16450.
48	4	3	8	17240.	16870.
49	4	3	9	17450.	16910.
50	3	2	10	16530.	16980.
51	1	4	7	17030.	17160.
52	4	4	7	17330.	17050.
53	2	5	4	17180.	17390.
54	3	4	3	17140.	17330.
55	2	1	4	19060.	17350.
56	1	3	2	17640.	17260.
57	3	3	2	18990.	17830.
58	6	1	7	19620.	18480.
59	3	1	9	20330.	18600.
60	1	3	7	19370.	19050.
61	2	3	6	20000.	19600.
62	1	4	3	18090.	19050.
63	3	3	3	20670.	19440.
64	2	1	4	17350.	19080.
65	3	3	4	19650.	19260.
66	2	2	4	20130.	19480.
67	3	1	6	21430.	20000.
68	2	1	7	22000.	20190.
69	1	1	7	19930.	20080.
70	4	2	9	22090.	20670.
71	2	5	6	21700.	21600.
72	1	3	4	21120.	21600.
73	2	4	2	20090.	20970.
74	2	2	2	20350.	20600.
75	3	1	4	22660.	20710.
76	1	0	5	0.	20710.
77	0	2	3	22030.	20710.
78	4	3	4	22780.	21990.
79	3	3	4	23080.	22760.
80	0	1	3	23700.	22800.
81	2	3	2	23860.	23280.
82	3	2	3	25610.	23850.
83	1	2	2	22710.	24030.
84	2	1	3	24580.	24070.
85	1	3	1	23590.	23850.
86	0	1	0	25380.	24240.
87	3	1	2	26670.	24400.
88	3	0	5	0.	24400.
89	3	1	7	25600.	24400.
90	4	0	11	0.	24400.
91	4	1	14	26840.	24520.
92	1	1	14	26980.	25300.
93	3	2	15	24740.	25170.
94	1	4	12	25230.	25650.
95	3	1	14	28210.	25800.
96	2	2	14	25590.	25670.
97	3	4	13	24240.	25300.

98	2	3	12	25590.	25310.
99	2	1	13	25990.	25090.
100	0	3	10	23360.	24160.
101	4	1	13	21450.	23970.
102	6	1	18	23150.	23910.
103	6	4	20	23030.	23280.
104	4	1	23	24100.	23090.
105	0	2	21	24620.	23240.
106	3	0	24	0.	23240.
107	1	2	23	25300.	23920.
108	2	1	24	23750.	23980.
109	2	1	25	26380.	24030.
110	3	2	26	24270.	24320.
111	1	3	24	24810.	24890.
112	2	4	22	24980.	24930.
113	2	3	21	25540.	25100.
114	1	2	20	24310.	24690.
115	2	3	19	20590.	23690.
116	2	5	16	21810.	21940.
117	7	4	19	22170.	21830.
118	1	6	14	22340.	22270.
119	1	4	11	22360.	22350.
120	1	2	10	21350.	21920.
121	3	3	10	19250.	20890.
122	1	2	9	19880.	20520.
123	4	2	11	20040.	20340.
124	4	0	15	0.	20340.
125	2	2	15	19320.	20080.
126	1	3	13	21830.	20160.
127	4	1	16	22180.	20610.
128	3	2	17	21730.	20980.
129	4	2	19	21770.	21330.
130	0	3	16	21760.	21780.
131	4	2	18	18130.	21070.
132	2	2	18	20460.	20770.
133	3	4	17	21930.	20760.
134	5	3	19	18450.	20210.
135	1	0	20	0.	20210.
136	2	2	20	19870.	20370.
137	0	2	18	21630.	20560.
138	6	4	20	20370.	20160.
139	3	4	19	17730.	19570.
140	1	4	16	19380.	19210.
141	1	3	14	18290.	18710.
142	1	2	13	19990.	18860.
143	1	3	11	19300.	19260.
144	3	3	11	19920.	19270.
145	0	2	9	20760.	19910.
146	1	4	6	18750.	19490.
147	1	2	5	19250.	19440.
148	2	3	4	21260.	19800.
149	4	2	6	19920.	19790.
150	4	6	4	19590.	19980.
151	1	2	3	21650.	20070.
152	3	0	6	0.	20070.
153	2	1	7	20480.	19940.
154	3	4	6	20800.	20750.

155	3	1	8	20750.	21080.
156	2	3	7	22910.	21510.
157	1	3	5	20960.	21360.
158	3	4	4	23420.	22530.
159	1	2	3	20280.	21950.
160	1	2	2	24210.	22490.
161	4	3	3	20480.	22060.
162	1	3	1	24240.	22310.
163	1	0	2	0.	22310.
164	1	0	3	0.	22310.
165	3	1	5	24540.	22660.
166	3	2	6	23790.	23040.
167	1	3	4	24440.	24290.
168	1	2	3	23940.	24180.
169	1	3	1	23100.	23800.
170	2	1	2	26180.	24070.
171	3	2	3	26470.	24420.
172	3	2	4	26870.	25000.
173	1	1	4	27500.	25360.
174	1	3	2	25930.	25910.
175	4	2	4	23780.	25950.
176	1	0	5	0.	25950.
177	1	1	5	27970.	26100.
178	2	0	7	0.	26100.
179	2	1	8	28710.	26320.
180	3	0	11	0.	26320.
181	2	2	11	28960.	26740.
182	5	0	16	0.	26740.
183	2	2	16	26820.	26940.
184	3	0	19	0.	26940.
185	2	1	20	28250.	27190.
186	2	2	20	27400.	27570.
187	0	1	19	26570.	27780.
188	3	3	19	25070.	26740.
189	3	2	20	29940.	26890.
190	1	3	18	25690.	26360.
191	2	3	17	27900.	26980.
192	4	2	19	20160.	26090.
193	2	4	17	25500.	24850.
194	2	3	16	22670.	23930.
195	0	2	14	27200.	24460.
196	2	2	14	23190.	24960.
197	3	4	13	24560.	24680.
198	5	2	16	23380.	24570.
199	2	0	18	0.	24570.
200	3	1	20	22500.	24180.
201	1	1	20	26590.	24040.
202	4	3	21	22230.	23330.
203	2	2	21	24330.	23280.
204	0	1	20	25400.	23660.
205	2	2	20	23000.	23580.
206	0	1	19	22310.	23560.
207	1	3	17	24160.	23580.
208	4	1	20	25940.	24080.
209	1	4	17	22920.	23490.
210	2	2	17	21100.	23230.
211	1	3	15	25430.	23610.

212	0	1	14	23920.	23410.
213	2	3	13	23310.	23500.
214	3	2	14	18630.	22710.
215	1	3	12	23580.	22710.
216	1	4	9	21380.	21420.
217	2	4	7	21000.	21490.
218	3	1	9	23830.	21340.
219	3	3	9	17650.	20470.
220	3	1	11	23010.	20330.
221	4	0	15	0.	20330.
222	1	2	14	22220.	20950.
223	2	2	14	23040.	21270.
224	2	2	14	23390.	21320.
225	2	2	14	20310.	21850.
226	6	4	16	23770.	22850.
227	0	2	14	21530.	22550.
228	2	4	12	20670.	22080.
229	1	3	10	21960.	21560.
230	0	4	6	19810.	20830.
231	5	3	8	19720.	20430.
232	2	3	7	18420.	19360.
233	5	2	10	21420.	19950.
234	3	1	12	21950.	20300.
235	2	2	12	22330.	20570.
236	4	2	14	21850.	20840.
237	2	2	14	21780.	21400.
238	3	3	14	22310.	22080.
239	0	4	10	20990.	21710.
240	1	2	9	19960.	21150.
241	3	2	10	21910.	21480.
242	4	3	11	21850.	21380.
243	0	2	9	21380.	21400.
244	4	5	8	19620.	20640.
245	0	3	5	20380.	20200.
246	3	2	6	19270.	19780.
247	2	0	8	0.	19780.
248	0	2	6	21290.	19980.
249	1	3	4	21260.	20600.
250	1	3	2	20450.	20620.

Table 2. Simulated Ghost Town Market

PROBABILITY OF LEAVING   .02
NUMBER SEEKING HOUSING   10
ACQUISITIVENESS*
PURCHASING POWER MEAN   17150.

---

* Acquisitiveness was set at 4 uniformly for all sellers during
  this experiment.

CYCLE NUMBER	EXIT RATE	ENTR RATE	TOTAL VACANT	AVERG COST	PRIC AVERG
					15000.
1	1	1	0	16500.	15150.
2	3	2	1	16660.	15480.
3	8	2	7	17030.	15880.
4	5	3	9	16710.	16400.
5	5	2	12	16730.	16740.
6	3	1	14	18420.	16940.
7	8	1	21	18630.	17130.
8	2	2	21	18260.	17420.
9	3	4	20	18980.	18290.
10	7	3	24	16590.	18080.
11	6	7	23	17790.	17430.
12	7	2	28	17560.	17710.
13	5	2	31	16470.	17740.
14	2	5	28	15810.	16300.
15	4	3	29	17880.	16560.
16	2	4	27	18200.	17510.
17	4	7	24	16380.	16870.
18	4	4	24	16480.	16260.
19	5	2	27	14490.	16030.
20	7	0	34	0.	16030.
21	0	2	32	17600.	16340.
22	3	2	33	17400.	16490.
23	3	5	31	17490.	16970.
24	0	3	28	16630.	17210.
25	7	5	30	17050.	17090.
26	3	2	31	18800.	17270.
27	2	2	31	19000.	17720.
28	0	4	27	16260.	17190.
29	7	2	32	16780.	17420.
30	4	6	30	15850.	16450.
31	8	2	36	13990.	15660.
32	5	3	38	14550.	15240.
33	3	4	37	17530.	15610.
34	4	3	38	13730.	15490.
35	3	2	39	16930.	16240.
36	4	3	40	16940.	16190.
37	5	6	39	13890.	15090.
38	5	5	39	15030.	14690.
39	5	1	43	17100.	14790.
40	4	4	43	15050.	15250.

41	5	4	44	15060.	14880.
42	5	4	45	14290.	14780.
43	3	4	44	14230.	14080.
44	4	5	43	14940.	14810.
45	7	4	46	15380.	15250.
46	4	2	48	16780.	15390.
47	4	5	47	15390.	15570.
48	4	7	44	14840.	14750.
49	5	2	47	13770.	14830.
50	2	7	42	14730.	13980.
51	2	4	40	13810.	14190.
52	5	5	40	13460.	13890.
53	4	1	43	14940.	13750.
54	4	4	43	13200.	13500.
55	7	4	46	14220.	13800.
56	2	6	42	12600.	13250.
57	5	1	46	11860.	12950.
58	3	6	43	11350.	12180.
59	2	6	39	9120.	10020.
60	3	1	41	13700.	10230.
61	4	4	41	12630.	10790.
62	5	1	45	13150.	11380.
63	1	3	43	12440.	12570.
64	4	6	41	12480.	12540.
65	3	5	39	12570.	12520.
66	3	2	40	12550.	12590.
67	3	4	39	13760.	12920.
68	4	6	37	12510.	13010.
69	5	3	39	11230.	12260.
70	3	5	37	11080.	11550.
71	4	5	36	9110.	10090.
72	2	5	33	11800.	10450.
73	2	4	31	11670.	11550.
74	5	3	33	12230.	11580.
75	6	3	36	11090.	11660.
76	6	3	39	12160.	11910.
77	0	1	38	9360.	11580.
78	2	4	36	11570.	11430.
79	4	7	33	11430.	11360.
80	2	1	34	12490.	11330.
81	3	4	33	12410.	11700.
82	5	2	36	11330.	12140.
83	2	4	34	10190.	11310.
84	3	5	32	11370.	10900.
85	1	4	29	11570.	11200.
86	5	4	30	9830.	11050.
87	4	3	31	11500.	11020.
88	0	5	26	9080.	10110.
89	6	3	29	8780.	9410.
90	2	3	28	10890.	9700.
91	3	3	28	10780.	10030.
92	3	2	29	8920.	9970.
93	7	1	35	6680.	9910.
94	4	2	37	10900.	10100.
95	3	5	35	7880.	8570.
96	4	1	38	10460.	8510.
97	3	0	41	0.	8510.

98	8	2	47	9620.	9090.
99	4	1	50	10230.	9020.
100	4	0	54	0.	9020.
101	2	1	55	9920.	8920.
102	3	2	56	9110.	9130.
103	6	2	60	9100.	9260.
104	4	1	63	9830.	9610.
105	1	3	61	9940.	9620.
106	2	0	63	0.	9620.
107	3	4	62	9650.	9640.
108	2	2	62	9990.	9820.
109	4	2	64	8590.	9500.
110	4	1	67	9000.	9440.
111	2	2	67	9440.	9300.
112	0	3	64	9080.	9220.
113	5	2	67	9150.	9060.
114	2	4	65	7790.	8710.
115	2	2	65	9360.	8770.
116	2	2	65	9430.	8700.
117	4	3	66	9490.	9010.
118	5	3	68	9910.	9580.
119	5	4	69	8540.	9230.
120	2	2	69	9650.	9270.
121	5	2	72	8400.	9010.
122	1	2	71	7790.	8580.
123	4	2	73	8000.	8490.
124	8	2	79	8930.	8550.
125	7	2	84	8600.	8340.
126	1	1	84	9220.	8600.
127	2	2	84	9120.	8760.
128	2	2	84	7940.	8460.
129	8	2	90	7420.	8490.
130	2	1	91	7720.	8310.
131	2	1	92	9150.	8440.
132	3	1	94	8140.	8320.
133	5	0	99	0.	8320.
134	5	2	102	9030.	8250.
135	5	1	106	4760.	7850.
136	2	2	106	8890.	8040.
137	3	2	107	7340.	8020.
138	4	1	110	8830.	8140.
139	2	1	111	8950.	8120.
140	0	1	110	8770.	8180.
141	2	1	111	9000.	8160.
142	2	1	112	8820.	8150.
143	1	0	113	0.	8150.
144	3	1	115	8970.	8580.
145	5	3	117	9100.	8910.
146	2	3	116	9610.	9170.
147	2	2	116	7330.	8850.
148	4	2	118	7630.	8600.
149	3	2	119	7490.	8210.
150	1	2	118	7960.	8040.
151	1	3	116	6680.	7350.
152	1	2	115	6040.	7110.
153	2	0	117	0.	7110.
154	3	1	119	8600.	7160.

155	3	2	120	6980.	7060.
156	1	1	120	8250.	6940.
157	1	3	118	5870.	6590.
158	2	1	119	7910.	6840.
159	1	1	119	7680.	6840.
160	2	1	120	7530.	7150.
161	1	0	121	0.	7150.
162	2	1	122	7060.	7000.
163	5	1	126	7070.	6910.
164	1	2	125	6320.	6750.
165	0	0	125	0.	6750.
166	1	1	125	6630.	6750.
167	1	1	125	7270.	6670.
168	3	1	127	7340.	7110.
169	3	0	130	0.	7110.
170	4	1	133	7820.	7100.
171	3	0	136	0.	7100.
172	1	1	136	7810.	7110.
173	4	0	140	0.	7110.
174	0	1	139	7660.	7130.
175	2	1	140	6900.	7110.
176	1	2	139	5820.	6810.
177	0	1	138	7520.	7060.
178	2	2	138	7760.	7220.
179	6	3	141	7590.	7200.
180	1	1	141	7920.	7220.
181	0	1	140	6910.	7230.
182	1	1	140	7950.	7240.
183	1	1	140	7960.	7650.
184	4	1	143	8420.	7740.
185	2	2	143	8520.	7890.
186	1	3	141	7160.	7770.
187	3	2	142	8540.	7990.
188	2	2	142	8790.	8160.
189	2	2	142	8580.	8180.
190	2	2	142	8210.	8280.
191	2	3	141	7890.	8330.
192	3	1	143	8640.	8340.
193	4	1	146	9180.	8380.
194	3	1	148	5800.	8080.
195	0	0	148	0.	8080.
196	1	3	146	7080.	7750.
197	3	0	149	0.	7750.
198	0	2	147	7960.	7710.
199	2	1	148	8480.	7830.
200	3	1	150	8310.	7750.
201	1	1	150	8530.	7740.
202	1	2	149	8390.	7920.
203	5	1	153	8710.	7900.
204	3	1	155	8690.	8420
205	0	1	154	8510.	8390.
206	1	0	155	0.	8390.
207	0	2	153	8600.	8520.
208	0	1	152	7840.	8450.
209	2	3	151	7260.	8100.
210	1	1	151	6610.	7930.
211	2	0	153	0.	7930.

212	5	0	158	0.	7930.
213	2	1	159	8720.	7930.
214	3	2	160	7820.	7780.
215	2	0	162	0.	7780.
216	2	0	164	0.	7780.
217	1	0	165	0.	7780.
218	2	1	166	8550.	7820.
219	1	1	166	5800.	7490.
220	1	0	167	0.	7490.
221	2	1	168	5560.	7260.
222	1	0	169	0.	7260.
223	2	2	169	7460.	7340.
224	0	0	169	0.	7340.
225	0	1	168	7670.	7340.
226	4	0	172	0.	7340.
227	1	0	173	0.	7340.
228	2	1	174	7910.	7470.
229	0	2	172	7440.	7400.
230	0	1	171	7750.	7300.
231	0	3	168	6600.	7290.
232	1	3	166	7130.	7170.
233	2	0	168	0.	7170.
234	1	1	168	7890.	7170.
235	0	0	168	0.	7170.
236	1	2	167	7650.	7210.
237	3	0	170	0.	7210.
238	0	0	170	0.	7210.
239	0	0	170	0.	7210.
240	2	3	169	7770.	7510.
241	1	0	170	0.	7510.
242	4	4	170	8210.	7930.
243	1	3	168	5870.	7370.
244	2	1	169	5080.	7140.
245	0	0	169	0.	7140.
246	2	1	170	5310.	6880.
247	1	2	169	7060.	6670.
248	1	0	170	0.	6670.
249	3	1	172	6180.	6460.
250	1	0	173	0.	6460.

Table 3. Simulated Boom Town Market

PROBABILITY OF LEAVING	.01
NUMBER SEEKING HOUSING	50
ACQUISITIVENESS*	
PURCHASING POWER MEAN	17150.

---

* Acquisitiveness was set at 4 uniformly for all
  sellers during this experiment.

CYCLE NUMBER	EXIT RATE	ENTR RATE	TOTAL VACANT	AVERG COST	PRIC AVERG
					15000.
1	1	1	0	16500.	15150.
2	3	3	0	16660.	15640.
3	4	4	0	17210.	16530.
4	0	0	0	0.	16530.
5	4	4	0	18180.	17480.
6	2	2	0	19230.	18000.
7	3	3	0	19800.	18770.
8	2	2	0	20650.	19370.
9	4	4	0	21300.	20510.
10	1	1	0	22560.	20840.
11	5	4	1	22930.	22010.
12	2	3	0	23630.	22770.
13	1	1	0	25050.	23150.
14	3	1	2	25460.	23560.
15	3	5	0	25530.	24900.
16	2	2	0	27390.	25540.
17	0	0	0	0.	25540.
18	2	2	0	28090.	26400.
19	2	2	0	29040.	27070.
20	2	2	0	29780.	27850.
21	7	2	5	30630.	28980.
22	4	2	7	31880.	29880.
23	3	3	7	29400.	30180.
24	3	7	3	31430.	30820.
25	1	4	0	31750.	31820.
26	2	1	1	35000.	32100.
27	0	1	0	34300.	32470.
28	1	1	0	35710.	33160.
29	5	3	2	36470.	34140.
30	3	3	2	37550.	35700.
31	3	3	2	36430.	36700.
32	1	3	0	39110.	37570.
33	3	0	3	0.	37570.
34	2	4	1	40910.	39030.
35	0	1	0	39690.	39490.
36	2	2	0	43440.	40750.
37	1	1	0	44830.	41200.
38	1	1	0	45320.	41880.
39	3	0	3	0.	41880.
40	1	4	0	45370.	43950.
41	1	0	1	0.	43950.
42	3	0	4	0.	43950.
43	2	2	4	48340.	45520.

44	2	1	5	46420.	45810.
45	1	0	6	0.	45810.
46	2	1	7	44580.	45930.
47	4	1	10	50520.	46500.
48	2	2	10	42370.	45830.
49	3	0	13	0.	45830.
50	2	0	15	0.	45830.
51	0	2	13	49400.	46680.
52	4	1	16	43720.	46540.
53	4	3	17	47170.	46380.
54	1	0	18	0.	46380.
55	2	2	18	47830.	46440.
56	4	3	19	41670.	45530.
57	4	2	21	42600.	44740.
58	3	3	21	39790.	42520.
59	2	0	23	0.	42520.
60	2	2	23	40280.	41010.
61	1	0	24	0.	41010.
62	2	1	25	45370.	41630.
63	3	0	28	0.	41630.
64	5	0	33	0.	41630.
65	1	0	34	0.	41630.
66	4	2	36	44880.	42020.
67	1	3	34	43680.	42570.
68	1	3	32	43080.	43150.
69	1	1	32	43090.	43850.
70	2	3	31	39870.	42300.
71	1	5	27	38650.	40120.
72	2	3	26	36160.	38080.
73	1	1	26	38140.	38210.
74	0	5	21	38620.	37520.
75	3	2	22	38050.	37690.
76	5	3	24	36880.	37980.
77	2	2	24	33340.	36920.
78	2	5	21	36700.	36080.
79	2	2	21	36060.	35630.
80	0	6	15	33760.	35460.
81	1	8	8	34310.	34480.
82	2	7	3	36040.	35160.
83	0	3	0	35080.	35750.
84	2	0	2	0.	35750.
85	1	1	2	39330.	35890.
86	5	2	5	37760.	36660.
87	2	1	6	40320.	37020.
88	1	1	6	40720.	37420.
89	0	2	4	37930.	37690.
90	4	2	6	38930.	38460.
91	1	3	4	39530.	39110.
92	3	3	4	37640.	38520.
93	1	2	3	42260.	39390.
94	2	3	2	39920.	39350.
95	5	1	6	43280.	39610.
96	3	2	7	41610.	40070.
97	2	0	9	0.	40070.
98	3	4	8	42450.	41600.
99	2	2	8	44470.	42850.
100	2	3	7	42150.	42480.

101	4	4	7	41020.	42130.
102	3	2	8	37540.	41140.
103	2	0	10	0.	41140.
104	2	2	10	45250.	41460.
105	2	1	11	43450.	41320.
106	2	1	12	42730.	41580.
107	4	0	16	0.	41580.
108	3	1	18	45740.	42400.
109	2	1	19	39260.	42180.
110	3	5	17	43050.	43170.
111	2	1	18	43040.	42950.
112	2	3	17	41890.	42320.
113	2	3	16	46460.	43060.
114	3	3	16	43190.	43760.
115	4	0	20	0.	43760.
116	2	3	19	42490.	43420.
117	2	3	18	39080.	42060.
118	1	4	15	36670.	39140.
119	5	4	16	34740.	35510.
120	0	1	15	31390.	35080.
121	2	3	14	42660.	36480.
122	2	2	14	39150.	37660.
123	1	1	14	41790.	38260.
124	2	1	15	42080.	38980.
125	3	5	13	39710.	40200.
126	2	2	13	36090.	39240.
127	1	3	11	39030.	38780.
128	7	3	15	36590.	38200.
129	1	4	12	38410.	38050.
130	3	1	14	41850.	38410.
131	2	1	15	33400.	37640.
132	1	1	15	32730.	37140.
133	1	1	15	36430.	37080.
134	2	1	16	39760.	37360.
135	1	1	16	41100.	37890.
136	6	4	18	40420.	38690.
137	3	2	19	42560.	39680.
138	3	4	18	43160.	41940.
139	2	4	16	37620.	40820.
140	2	3	15	34250.	38220.
141	7	1	21	44300.	38290.
142	1	5	17	34140.	35700.
143	6	4	19	39370.	37250.
144	1	5	15	34560.	36710.
145	1	4	12	36510.	36110.
146	1	3	10	35090.	34360.
147	4	2	12	38850.	35960.
148	4	5	11	38430.	37510.
149	2	2	11	37240.	38230.
150	1	5	7	38800.	38400.
151	1	1	7	42240.	38980.
152	0	1	6	34130.	38440.
153	1	1	6	32050.	37690.
154	0	2	4	32270.	36690.
155	1	5	0	34650.	34620.
156	2	0	2	0.	34620.
157	1	1	2	38080.	34200.

158	4	2	4	37620.	35110.
159	2	0	6	0.	35110.
160	7	3	10	36690.	35600.
161	3	3	10	39160.	37160.
162	0	6	4	36510.	37440.
163	1	1	4	33020.	36960.
164	4	6	2	38000.	36890.
165	4	2	4	40200.	37850.
166	2	0	6	0.	37850.
167	3	1	8	38960.	38040.
168	2	1	9	40790.	38810.
169	2	3	8	41790.	40170.
170	10	0	18	0.	40170.
171	2	1	19	39370.	40040.
172	2	3	18	36020.	39240.
173	6	6	18	38040.	37570.
174	3	1	20	42290.	37860.
175	1	0	21	0.	37860.
176	2	1	22	41650.	38170.
177	5	3	24	41590.	40250.
178	2	2	24	41150.	40640.
179	1	3	22	42800.	41940.
180	2	2	22	41880.	41920.
181	4	5	21	37680.	40050.
182	1	3	19	41800.	39750.
183	5	3	21	34580.	38080.
184	2	4	19	33770.	36420.
185	3	2	20	32560.	33990.
186	2	4	18	35100.	34060.
187	2	3	17	34440.	34260.
188	2	2	17	35310.	34690.
189	5	3	19	35370.	34930.
190	0	2	17	35950.	35190.
191	3	2	18	36630.	36270.
192	2	3	17	35000.	35630.
193	4	5	16	38080.	36870.
194	4	6	14	37910.	38070.
195	2	7	9	38630.	38600.
196	5	1	13	33580.	37900.
197	4	3	14	35510.	36870.
198	3	6	11	33020.	33830.
199	2	3	10	36720.	34070.
200	1	3	8	38590.	36050.
201	4	3	9	37040.	36850.
202	0	3	6	38860.	38350.
203	1	5	2	37860.	38120.
204	1	1	2	41930.	38740.
205	1	1	2	42620.	39040.
206	1	2	1	34460.	38160.
207	4	0	5	0.	38160.
208	1	1	5	41970.	38470.
209	2	1	6	40400.	38830.
210	2	1	7	42710.	39410.
211	5	1	11	41850.	39380.
212	4	2	13	38870.	39810.
213	7	3	17	39990.	39910.
214	4	3	18	40630.	40410.

215	3	1	20	39980.	40140.
216	3	0	23	0.	40140.
217	2	2	23	39200.	39810.
218	1	3	21	41560.	40400.
219	2	2	21	44440.	41220.
220	1	4	18	37910.	39940.
221	1	3	16	41860.	40930.
222	0	0	16	0.	40930.
223	1	5	12	36560.	38520.
224	1	4	9	36950.	37450.
225	1	3	7	35220.	35970.
226	3	2	8	37150.	36170.
227	3	10	1	37030.	37030.
228	2	1	2	40740.	37630.
229	5	2	5	39310.	38320.
230	2	1	6	40560.	38390.
231	3	2	7	40280.	38490.
232	3	2	8	41860.	40250.
233	2	1	9	44270.	40800.
234	3	3	9	43470.	42090.
235	2	4	7	40420.	42010.
236	5	4	8	40410.	40880.
237	1	4	5	44510.	42490.
238	0	2	3	39420.	41850.
239	2	3	2	41100.	42180.
240	2	1	3	46400.	42660.
241	4	2	5	42830.	42470.
242	1	2	4	45640.	42540.
243	5	0	9	0.	42540.
244	4	1	12	45860.	42690.
245	2	0	14	0.	42690.
246	0	1	13	46020.	43850.
247	2	2	13	44560.	45030.
248	2	0	15	0.	45030.
249	2	1	16	41430.	44570.
250	4	2	18	41010.	43990.

Table 4.   Another "Normal Market

```
    PROBABILITY OF LEAVING                  .01
    NUMBER SEEKING HOUSING                   10
    ACQUISITIVENESS*
    PURCHASING POWER MEAN                 17150.
```

---

* Acquisitiveness was set at 4 uniformly for all
  sellers during this experiment.

CYCLE NUMBER	EXIT RATE	ENTR RATE	TOTAL VACANT	AVERG COST	PRIC AVERG
					15000.
1	2	2	0	16500.	15300.
2	7	0	7	0.	15300.
3	0	0	7	0.	15300.
4	4	3	8	16830.	15840.
5	3	3	8	16580.	16320.
6	1	3	6	16320.	16570.
7	4	4	6	16710.	16550.
8	2	3	5	17100.	16710.
9	3	5	3	17440.	17190.
10	4	0	7	0.	17190.
11	1	3	5	15850.	16780.
12	2	0	7	0.	16780.
13	3	0	10	0.	16780.
14	2	2	10	17750.	17020.
15	2	1	11	18730.	17440.
16	3	2	12	18030.	17460.
17	2	4	10	18990.	18300.
18	4	2	12	17230.	18290.
19	3	3	12	17700.	18120.
20	2	0	14	0.	18120.
21	2	3	13	18370.	18060.
22	1	3	11	19310.	18450.
23	5	4	12	18060.	18530.
24	3	5	10	16540.	17450.
25	1	3	8	19120.	17700.
26	2	2	8	13620.	16730.
27	1	2	7	19120.	17300.
28	3	3	7	19030.	17990.
29	0	1	6	18310.	17830.
30	3	4	5	18530.	18770.
31	0	2	3	18080.	18570.
32	3	1	5	16890.	18350.
33	4	2	7	18370.	18220.
34	3	3	7	18760.	18300.
35	4	1	10	20130.	18580.
36	5	1	14	20440.	18660.
37	1	2	13	20280.	19100.
38	3	4	12	19960.	20100.
39	2	1	13	22110.	20310.
40	3	3	13	20220.	20320.
41	3	5	11	20220.	20480.
42	1	3	9	21260.	20320.
43	2	6	5	19030.	20030.

44	0	1	4	16130.	19410.
45	2	5	1	19120.	18250.
46	4	2	3	17700.	18460.
47	3	3	3	20090.	19120.
48	4	3	4	20060.	19850.
49	4	2	6	20360.	19660.
50	3	4	5	21260.	20560.
51	3	3	5	22070.	21120.
52	5	3	7	22870.	21980.
53	8	1	14	20130.	21830.
54	6	1	19	24020.	22070.
55	4	2	21	21250.	22140.
56	1	3	19	19400.	21340.
57	2	1	20	23870.	21410.
58	2	3	19	22070.	21480.
59	3	2	20	22510.	21150.
60	1	1	20	23270.	21650.
61	7	3	24	22430.	22560.
62	1	2	23	21140.	22050.
63	2	0	25	0.	22050.
64	3	0	28	0.	22050.
65	5	3	30	21270.	21800.
66	1	4	27	19580.	20710.
67	4	4	27	22150.	21030.
68	1	1	27	17790.	20890.
69	0	1	26	22670.	20740.
70	5	2	29	22810.	21300.
71	2	4	27	21350.	21820.
72	2	2	27	21250.	21400.
73	2	4	25	20430.	20960.
74	2	6	21	18590.	19320.
75	4	1	24	17890.	19100.
76	2	1	25	22130.	19160.
77	4	4	25	17970.	18750.
78	2	4	23	18480.	18580.
79	2	2	23	16210.	17820.
80	1	7	17	17700.	17630.
81	2	2	17	18260.	17860.
82	5	3	19	17910.	17340.
83	4	5	18	18240.	18140.
84	3	6	15	18390.	18510.
85	0	2	13	18480.	18470.
86	4	2	15	18720.	18470.
87	2	4	13	20110.	19060.
88	2	4	11	19430.	19560.
89	5	2	14	19180.	19650.
90	6	2	18	18790.	19350.
91	1	2	17	16180.	18600.
92	5	2	20	18350.	18540.
93	0	5	15	18270.	18200.
94	2	4	13	18640.	18170.
95	0	2	11	14560.	17470.
96	1	1	11	14260.	17370.
97	5	2	14	19110.	17640.
98	2	2	14	19410.	17530.
99	3	1	16	19280.	17970.
100	2	3	15	17880.	17870.

101	2	2	15	18490.	18690.
102	2	4	13	18730.	18480.
103	5	3	15	17660.	18280.
104	0	3	12	18040.	18200.
105	2	3	11	18400.	18290.
106	2	3	10	18190.	18020.
107	1	1	10	19820.	18370.
108	1	1	10	14570.	18230.
109	2	2	10	16190.	17650.
110	1	3	8	15340.	16730.
111	3	3	8	17110.	16410.
112	2	2	8	18740.	16720.
113	2	1	9	18240.	16880.
114	2	1	10	18560.	17160.
115	0	1	9	18180.	17580.
116	4	1	12	17290.	17500.
117	4	2	14	18090.	18360.
118	2	3	13	17030.	17820.
119	1	5	9	16830.	17140.
120	4	1	12	15310.	16980.
121	1	1	12	18680.	16920.
122	1	3	10	17170.	16970.
123	1	3	8	17080.	17080.
124	4	2	10	18080.	17290.
125	1	1	10	17910.	17550.
126	2	3	9	18120.	17420.
127	1	1	9	19160.	17880.
128	1	2	8	18770.	18290.
129	0	2	6	15360.	17850.
130	2	4	4	18120.	17570.
131	2	1	5	16280.	17620.
132	4	3	6	16090.	16770.
133	4	5	5	17830.	17030.
134	1	2	4	18400.	17420.
135	2	3	3	18700.	18210.
136	4	1	6	20030.	18310.
137	2	3	5	18920.	18870.
138	0	3	2	18530.	18850.
139	2	0	4	0.	18850.
140	3	2	5	20730.	19160.
141	2	2	5	18370.	19050.
142	4	3	6	19390.	19190.
143	2	0	8	0.	19190.
144	1	0	9	0.	19190.
145	3	0	12	0.	19190.
146	5	1	16	17970.	19020.
147	1	3	14	20480.	19500.
148	2	3	13	20380.	19870.
149	2	3	12	18420.	19580.
150	3	2	13	21540.	20000.
151	3	1	15	22000.	20210.
152	1	4	12	19490.	19830.
153	0	4	8	20360.	20290.
154	2	3	7	21460.	20550.
155	1	3	5	19240.	20350.
156	2	4	3	18060.	19430.
157	4	3	4	19570.	18860.

158	3	2	5	18020.	18960.
159	2	2	5	20850.	19180.
160	2	1	6	19920.	19490.
161	1	2	5	21050.	19840.
162	5	3	7	20980.	20270.
163	3	1	9	19840.	20160.
164	2	4	7	21170.	20960.
165	1	1	7	21400.	20950.
166	1	2	6	17620.	20230.
167	1	4	3	21660.	20580.
168	2	4	1	21180.	20660.
169	2	1	2	18920.	20790.
170	0	1	1	22260.	21250.
171	6	1	6	21810.	21170.
172	0	1	5	22910.	21490.
173	1	0	6	0.	21490.
174	1	0	7	0.	21490.
175	3	1	9	21560.	21430.
176	1	2	8	22340.	21420.
177	4	2	10	21230.	21720.
178	1	2	9	22000.	21970.
179	2	3	8	21690.	21780.
180	3	2	9	21200.	21500.
181	3	0	12	0.	21500.
182	2	1	13	21260.	21520.
183	4	3	14	22470.	21790.
184	3	3	14	22990.	21990.
185	2	3	13	21150.	22110.
186	3	1	15	24320.	22410.
187	3	0	18	0.	22410.
188	2	3	17	23130.	22610.
189	3	4	16	23370.	23060.
190	4	2	18	25370.	23790.
191	2	3	17	20170.	22940.
192	8	1	24	22250.	22700.
193	4	4	24	23390.	22700.
194	2	3	23	24800.	23140.
195	1	4	20	22080.	23120.
196	1	2	19	19130.	22590.
197	2	1	20	24920.	22590.
198	3	4	19	19070.	20490.
199	1	6	14	18950.	18990.
200	2	2	14	22750.	19790.
201	0	0	14	0.	19790.
202	3	0	17	0.	19790.
203	1	3	15	19820.	20190.
204	1	2	14	21700.	20330.
205	1	3	12	21090.	21160.
206	4	4	12	21280.	21140.
207	1	3	10	21910.	21410.
208	1	5	6	21140.	21540.
209	0	2	4	18350.	20810.
210	1	4	1	17470.	18870.
211	6	1	6	22430.	18880.
212	3	0	9	0.	18880.
213	1	1	9	20350.	18990.
214	2	3	8	20430.	19180.

215	1	3	6	20050.	19910.
216	3	0	9	0.	19910.
217	4	2	11	20330.	20490.
218	3	0	14	0.	20490.
219	2	6	10	19890.	19910.
220	2	3	9	20350.	19920.
221	1	3	7	21430.	20420.
222	2	2	7	19520.	20450.
223	1	2	6	22250.	20890.
224	9	1	14	19930.	21150.
225	1	3	12	21460.	21020.
226	4	4	12	21800.	21600.
227	3	1	14	22650.	21620.
228	1	4	11	21430.	21810.
229	3	3	11	23990.	22650.
230	2	3	10	17740.	21090.
231	4	2	12	24420.	21850.
232	4	4	12	22250.	21510.
233	1	1	12	23660.	21470.
234	1	4	9	21030.	22120.
235	3	2	10	20460.	21370.
236	1	1	10	17970.	21020.
237	6	1	15	20530.	20670.
238	2	5	12	21200.	20410.
239	4	3	13	20160.	20500.
240	3	2	14	20920.	20830.
241	3	2	15	22500.	20760.
242	2	0	17	0.	20760.
243	3	2	18	21530.	21330.
244	5	3	20	23460.	21890.
245	1	4	17	21030.	22050.
246	2	4	15	21810.	21830.
247	1	3	13	21610.	21630.
248	2	2	13	22710.	21780.
249	4	3	14	19810.	21320.
250	0	2	12	21270.	21220.

Table 5. A Color-Blind Neighborhood

PROBABILITY OF LEAVING   .01

NUMBER OF NEGROES SEEKING HOUSING   10

NUMBER OF WHITES SEEKING HOUSING   20

LEVEL OF ACQUISITIVENESS FOR BOTH   1

LEVEL OF PREJUDICE FOR WHITES   0

NEGRO PURCHASING POWER MEAN   14760

WHITE PURCHASING POWER MEAN   14760

CYCLE NUMBR	NEGRO LEAVE	WHITE LEAVE	NEGRO ENTER	WHITE ENTER	TOTAL VACNT	AVERG COST	PRIC AVERG	PROP NEGRO	SEGRE INDEX
1	0	2	1	1	0	15370.	15000.	0.0042	0.00
2	0	3	1	2	0	16010.	15070.	0.0083	1.00
3	0	2	1	1	0	16350.	15390.	0.0125	1.00
4	0	1	0	1	0	16450.	15660.	0.0125	1.00
5	0	3	1	2	0	16590.	15810.	0.0167	1.00
6	0	4	3	1	0	17150.	16210.	0.0292	1.00
7	0	2	0	2	0	17080.	16660.	0.0292	1.00
8	0	0	0	0	0	0.	16810.	0.0292	1.00
9	0	2	0	0	2	0.	16810.	0.0292	1.00
10	0	2	1	3	0	17700.	17230.	0.0333	1.00
11	0	2	1	1	0	17870.	17440.	0.0375	-0.07
12	0	2	1	1	0	17880.	17570.	0.0417	-0.05
13	0	4	2	2	0	18340.	17960.	0.0500	0.03
14	0	1	1	0	0	19310.	18170.	0.0542	0.18
15	0	3	3	0	0	19070.	18560.	0.0667	0.47
16	0	1	1	0	0	19490.	18720.	0.0708	0.53
17	1	0	0	0	0	0.	18720.	0.0708	0.53
18	1	3	1	1	2	19660.	19110.	0.0708	0.53
19	0	1	1	1	2	20540.	19530.	0.0708	0.53
20	1	3	2	3	0	19740.	19910.	0.0792	0.63
21	0	3	0	1	3	20410.	20000.	0.0750	0.58
22	0	1	1	3	0	20730.	20310.	0.0792	0.63
23	0	5	2	1	2	20930.	20870.	0.0875	0.70
24	0	1	3	1	0	21600.	21110.	0.1000	0.07
25	0	1	1	0	0	22170.	21280.	0.1042	0.15

CYCLE NUMBR	NEGRO LEAVE	WHITE LEAVE	NEGRO ENTER	WHITE ENTER	TOTAL VACNT	AVERG COST	PRIC AVERG	PROP NEGRO	SEGRE INDEX
26	0	2	0	2	0	22610.	21710.	0.1042	0.15
27	0	0	0	0	0	0.	21710.	0.1042	0.15
28	0	1	1	0	0	22790.	21790.	0.1083	-0.03
29	0	2	0	2	0	23420.	22310.	0.1083	-0.03
30	0	3	3	0	0	23610.	22970.	0.1208	-0.05
31	0	2	1	1	0	24410.	23450.	0.1250	-0.04
32	2	2	2	2	0	24030.	23920.	0.1250	-0.04
33	0	3	0	1	2	24510.	24020.	0.1250	-0.04
34	0	5	2	1	4	24610.	24320.	0.1333	-0.01
35	1	1	1	1	3	24540.	24350.	0.1375	0.03
36	0	5	1	1	7	24290.	24400.	0.1375	0.15
37	0	0	0	3	4	24670.	24550.	0.1375	0.15
38	0	4	1	1	6	25160.	24660.	0.1417	0.09
39	0	0	1	3	2	24040.	24470.	0.1458	0.14
40	1	1	0	3	0	24880.	24580.	0.1458	0.14
41	0	2	2	1	0	25800.	24820.	0.1500	-0.00
42	0	0	0	0	0		24820.	0.1500	-0.00
43	0	2	1	1	0	25750.	25180.	0.1542	-0.04
44	0	3	0	2	1	26120.	25580.	0.1542	0.04
45	0	5	1	0	5	26220.	25720.	0.1583	-0.02
46	0	4	0	1	8	25460.	25790.	0.1583	-0.02
47	0	2	2	1	7	25810.	25940.	0.1667	-0.02
48	0	4	0	2	9	25080.	25710.	0.1667	0.02
49	0	2	0	1	10	25220.	25680.	0.1667	0.02
50	1	1	0	3	9	25930.	25620.	0.1625	-0.01

CYCLE NUMBR	NEGRO LEAVE	WHITE LEAVE	NEGRO ENTER	WHITE ENTER	TOTAL VACNT	AVERG COST	PRIC AVERG	PROP NEGRO	SEGRE INDEX
51	1	0	0	2	8	24960.	25490.	0.1583	-0.02
52	0	1	0	3	6	24880.	25260.	0.1583	-0.02
53	1	1	2	3	3	25600.	25280.	0.1625	-0.03
54	1	1	1	1	3	25510.	25390.	0.1625	-0.01
55	0	4	0	2	5	25460.	25490.	0.1625	-0.01
56	0	3	0	4	4	26030.	25690.	0.1625	-0.03
57	0	3	0	1	8	26970.	25860.	0.1542	-0.06
58	2	3	0	3	5	25580.	25880.	0.1625	-0.08
59	0	2	2	2	1	25970.	25860.	0.1708	-0.05
60	0	0	0	0	2		25860.	0.1708	-0.05
61	0	1	1	1	4	25600.	25790.	0.1708	-0.07
62	1	3	1	2	1	26330.	25980.	0.1750	-0.10
63	0	0	1	2	1	26340.	26260.	0.1750	-0.16
64	1	2	1	1	5	26910.	26350.	0.1750	-0.16
65	1	5	0	2	5	26470.	26570.	0.1750	-0.16
66	0	2	2	2	6	27840.	26850.	0.1750	-0.16
67	1	3	0	3	6	26210.	26850.	0.1792	-0.18
68	2	3	0	1	6	27080.	26700.	0.1708	-0.19
69	0	1	1	1	10	26240.	26880.	0.1708	-0.19
70	0	5	0	0	9	26510.	26800.	0.1750	-0.20
71	0	1	0	1	11	0.	26530.	0.1750	-0.20
72	1	2	0	1	13	25850.	26530.	0.1708	-0.19
73	1	2	1	2	15	25440.	26380.	0.1708	-0.19
74	0	3	1	1	15	24950.	25770.	0.1750	-0.20
75	0	1	1	1	14	25520.	25580.	0.1792	-0.22

CYCLE NUMBR	NEGRO LEAVE	WHITE LEAVE	NEGRO ENTER	WHITE ENTER	TOTAL VACNT	AVERG COST	PRIC AVERG	PROP NEGRO	SEGRE INDEX
76	1	3	0	4	14	24210.	25240.	0.1750	-0.21
77	0	6	1	1	18	25230.	25260.	0.1792	-0.22
78	0	1	1	1	17	25430.	25320.	0.1833	-0.18
79	0	2	0	1	18	24640.	25250.	0.1875	-0.18
80	0	3	1	4	16	24530.	24830.	0.1875	-0.17
81	0	3	1	5	13	24270.	24480.	0.1917	-0.17
82	1	1	1	2	12	25550.	24820.	0.1917	-0.15
83	1	1	0	3	11	24520.	24920.	0.1875	-0.15
84	1	2	1	0	13	24350.	24910.	0.1875	-0.19
85	0	1	2	2	10	24670.	24660.	0.1958	-0.22
86	1	3	0	4	10	24650.	24620.	0.1917	-0.21
87	0	3	0	0	13	0.	24620.	0.1917	-0.21
88	0	0	1	4	8	24620.	24800.	0.1958	-0.22
89	2	1	1	3	7	25280.	24940.	0.1917	-0.22
90	0	2	2	2	6	24300.	25030.	0.1958	-0.22
91	0	3	2	2	5	25320.	25240.	0.2042	-0.22
92	0	0	0	0	5	0.	25240.	0.2042	-0.22
93	2	2	2	1	6	25250.	25080.	0.2042	-0.21
94	0	1	1	1	5	25260.	25160.	0.2083	-0.22
95	1	2	1	0	7	25350.	25280.	0.2083	-0.19
96	0	2	0	3	6	25060.	25200.	0.2083	-0.17
97	1	1	2	2	4	25420.	25270.	0.2125	-0.16
98	0	1	0	2	3	25560.	25330.	0.2125	-0.16
99	1	2	1	3	2	25440.	25480.	0.2125	-0.16
100	0	2	0	0	4	0.	25480.	0.2125	-0.16

CYCLE NUMBR	NEGRO LEAVE	WHITE LEAVE	NEGRO ENTER	WHITE ENTER	TOTAL VACNT	AVERG COST	PRIC AVERG	PROP NEGRO	SEGRE INDEX
101	0	3	3	1	3	25740.	25650.	0.2250	-0.11
102	0	2	2	1	2	26400.	25910.	0.2333	-0.11
103	0	2	1	2	1	26430.	26180.	0.2375	-0.09
104	0	3	0	4	0	26960.	26620.	0.2375	-0.09
105	1	4	0	1	4	27950.	26800.	0.2333	-0.11
106	0	7	0	3	8	27410.	27160.	0.2333	-0.13
107	1	2	3	1	7	27290.	27300.	0.2417	-0.14
108	1	2	0	0	10	0.	27300.	0.2375	-0.14
109	0	0	0	0	10	0.	27300.	0.2375	-0.14
110	1	1	0	4	8	26160.	26810.	0.2333	-0.13
111	1	2	1	2	8	26770.	26460.	0.2333	-0.13
112	1	1	1	0	9	27120.	26470.	0.2333	-0.11
113	1	3	0	2	11	27170.	26430.	0.2292	-0.11
114	0	2	1	3	10	26000.	26380.	0.2292	-0.09
115	0	0	0	3	7	26360.	26470.	0.2292	-0.08
116	3	0	1	2	4	26190.	26220.	0.2333	-0.08
117	0	0	1	1	5	25640.	26180.	0.2250	-0.03
118	0	4	1	0	8	26000.	26150.	0.2292	-0.03
119	0	1	2	2	5	26300.	26190.	0.2375	-0.02
120	2	2	1	1	5	26070.	26070.	0.2417	-0.03
121	1	2	2	2	5	25830.	26080.	0.2417	-0.02
122	0	2	1	1	6	26410.	26150.	0.2417	-0.03
123	3	3	1	2	6	26250.	26260.	0.2458	-0.04
124	1	3	0	3	9	26200.	26260.	0.2333	-0.05
125		0	1	0	9	25750.	26260.	0.2333	-0.05

CYCLE NUMBR	NEGRO LEAVE	WHITE LEAVE	NEGRO ENTER	WHITE ENTER	TOTAL VACNT	AVERG COST	PRIC AVERG	PROP NEGRO	SEGRE INDEX
126	0	4	0	3	10	25690.	26030.	0.2333	-0.05
127	0	2	3	0	9	25570.	25810.	0.2458	-0.05
128	1	2	2	1	9	25770.	25680.	0.2500	-0.04
129	0	2	0	1	10	25750.	25680.	0.2500	-0.02
130	0	0	1	1	8	25440.	25650.	0.2542	-0.01
131	0	2	0	2	8	25570.	25630.	0.2542	-0.01
132	0	3	1	3	7	25100.	25420.	0.2583	0.02
133	2	1	1	3	6	25540.	25450.	0.2542	0.06
134	0	1	0	3	4	25820.	25590.	0.2542	0.06
135	0	2	1	4	1	25680.	25930.	0.2583	0.02
136	0	1	1	1	0	27270.	26200.	0.2625	0.05
137	0	1	0	1	0	26860.	26310.	0.2625	0.05
138	1	2	0	1	2	26970.	26420.	0.2583	0.05
139	0	0	1	3	0	27070.	26740.	0.2625	0.05
140	1	3	0	1	1	28300.	27430.	0.2583	0.05
141	1	1	0	2	2	28110.	27550.	0.2542	-0.01
142	1	4	0	1	5	27640.	27620.	0.2500	-0.02
143	0	2	0	1	7	27730.	27710.	0.2458	-0.02
144	1	1	0	1	7	27670.	27780.	0.2458	-0.02
145	1	4	2	1	9	27650.	27900.	0.2500	-0.02
146	1	5	2	2	12	27080.	27510.	0.2500	-0.05
147	1	3	1	1	15	27170.	27520.	0.2458	-0.05
148	2	0	0	0	16	27240.	27420.	0.2417	-0.03
149	0	2	1	4	12	27310.	27220.	0.2500	-0.02
150	0	1	2	0	13	0.	27220.	0.2500	-0.02

Table 6. An Economically Segregated Neighborhood

PROBABILITY OF LEAVNING   .01

NUMBER OF NEGROES SEEKING HOUSING   10

NUMBER OF WHITES SEEKING HOUSING   20

LEVEL OF ACQUISITIVENESS FOR BOTH   1

LEVEL OF PREJUDICE FOR WHITES   0

NEGRO PURCHASING POWER MEAN   10400

WHITE PURCHASING POWER MEAN   14760

CYCLE NUMBR	NEGRO LEAVE	WHITE LEAVE	NEGRO ENTER	WHITE ENTER	TOTAL VACNT	AVERG COST	PRIC AVERG	PROP NEGRO	SEGRE INDEX
1	0	4	1	3	0	15680.	15000.	0.0042	0.00
2	0	4	2	1	1	16110.	15260.	0.0125	1.00
3	0	1	0	2	0	16140.	15600.	0.0125	1.00
4	0	2	0	2	0	16620.	15830.	0.0125	1.00
5	0	3	0	3	0	16880.	16080.	0.0125	1.00
6	0	3	1	1	1	17070.	16460.	0.0167	1.00
7	0	1	0	1	1	17150.	16630.	0.0167	1.00
8	0	0	1	0	0	17110.	16740.	0.0208	1.00
9	1	6	1	4	2	17330.	16860.	0.0208	1.00
10	0	6	1	4	0	17670.	17380.	0.0250	1.00
11	0	3	1	0	0	18620.	17730.	0.0292	1.00
12	0	1	1	1	0	18800.	17910.	0.0333	1.00
13	0	2	1	2	1	19210.	18080.	0.0333	1.00
14	0	3	0	2	0	18840.	18380.	0.0333	1.00
15	0	1	0	0	0	0.	18680.	0.0333	1.00
16	0	0	0	0	0	0.	18680.	0.0333	1.00
17	0	6	0	3	3	19300.	18680.	0.0333	1.00
18	0	3	2	4	0	20040.	19020.	0.0417	1.00
19	0	0	0	0	0	0.	19570.	0.0417	1.00
20	0	1	0	1	0	20060.	19570.	0.0417	1.00
21	0	3	0	3	0	20500.	19690.	0.0417	1.00
22	0	1	0	1	0	21550.	20050.	0.0417	1.00
23	2	2	0	2	0	21300.	20280.	0.0417	1.00
24	2	5	2	1	4	21550.	20530.	0.0417	1.00
25	0	4	1	3	4	21260.	20980.	0.0458	1.00

CYCLE NUMBR	NEGRO LEAVE	WHITE LEAVE	NEGRO ENTER	WHITE ENTER	TOTAL VACNT	AVERG COST	PRIC AVERG	PROP NEGRO	SEGRE INDEX
26	0	3	1	1	5	21290.	21380.	0.0500	1.00
27	0	6	2	5	4	21830.	21680.	0.0583	0.30
28	0	5	1	4	4	22300.	22210.	0.0625	0.39
29	1	1	1	2	3	22360.	22330.	0.0625	0.39
30	0	2	0	2	3	22960.	22430.	0.0625	0.39
31	0	0	0	0	3	0.	22430.	0.0625	0.39
32	0	5	0	3	5	22100.	22390.	0.0625	0.39
33	0	4	1	3	5	22580.	22590.	0.0667	0.47
34	0	1	1	2	3	22850.	22610.	0.0708	0.53
35	0	1	1	3	0	22870.	22900.	0.0750	0.58
36	1	3	0	3	1	23470.	23050.	0.0708	0.53
37	0	4	1	1	3	23750.	23230.	0.0750	0.58
38	0	0	0	2	1	23870.	23440.	0.0750	0.58
39	0	0	0	1	0	23350.	23500.	0.0750	0.58
40	0	3	1	2	0	25260.	24130.	0.0792	0.63
41	0	1	0	1	0	24130.	24190.	0.0792	0.63
42	0	5	0	1	4	24190.	24210.	0.0792	0.63
43	0	0	0	1	3	24190.	24260.	0.0792	0.63
44	0	2	0	2	3	24930.	24490.	0.0792	0.63
45	0	1	0	1	3	23720.	24460.	0.0792	0.63
46	0	5	0	4	4	24560.	24430.	0.0792	0.63
47	0	1	0	1	4	25040.	24520.	0.0792	0.63
48	0	0	1	2	1	24710.	24660.	0.0792	0.66
49	0	1	0	0	2	0.	24660.	0.0833	0.66
50	0	5	0	1	6	23270.	24440.	0.0833	0.66

CYCLE NUMBR	NEGRO LEAVE	WHITE LEAVE	NEGRO ENTER	WHITE ENTER	TOTAL VACNT	NEGRO AVCOS	PRIC AVERG	PROP NEGRO	SEGRE INDEX
51	0	3	0	1	8	0.	24550.	0.0833	0.66
52	0	2	0	1	9	0.	24730.	0.0833	0.66
53	2	2	1	1	11	24360.	24640.	0.0792	0.63
54	1	2	0	4	10	0.	24460.	0.0750	0.58
55	0	3	1	4	8	24040.	24340.	0.0792	0.25
56	0	3	0	2	9	0.	24380.	0.0792	0.25
57	0	1	0	1	9	0.	24270.	0.0792	0.25
58	0	4	0	2	11	0.	24090.	0.0792	0.25
59	1	2	1	3	10	25900.	24200.	0.0792	0.25
60	1	3	1	3	10	23950.	24250.	0.0792	-0.02
61	0	1	1	3	7	24900.	24290.	0.0833	-0.00
62	0	2	0	1	8	0.	24250.	0.0833	-0.00
63	0	2	0	0	10	0.	24250.	0.0833	-0.00
64	1	4	0	1	14	0.	24140.	0.0792	-0.02
65	1	1	0	2	14	0.	23790.	0.0750	0.16
66	0	2	0	3	13	0.	23780.	0.0750	0.16
67	0	1	0	3	11	0.	23560.	0.0750	0.16
68	0	2	1	3	9	21720.	23460.	0.0792	-0.02
69	0	4	0	1	12	0.	23460.	0.0792	-0.02
70	0	1	0	1	12	0.	23170.	0.0792	-0.02
71	1	1	0	3	11	0.	22750.	0.0750	-0.04
72	0	2	0	1	12	0.	22800.	0.0750	-0.04
73	0	3	0	0	15	0.	22800.	0.0750	-0.04
74	0	2	0	2	15	0.	22690.	0.0750	-0.04
75	0	1	2	3	11	21780.	22350.	0.0833	-0.00

CYCLE NUMBR	NEGRO LEAVE	WHITE LEAVE	NEGRO ENTER	WHITE ENTER	TOTAL VACNT	AVERG COST	PRIC AVERG	PROP NEGRO	SEGRE INDEX
76	1	4	0	3	13	22820.	22280.	0.0792	-0.02
77	0	2	1	4	10	22450.	22360.	0.0833	-0.00
78	0	3	1	5	7	22470.	22500.	0.0875	-0.03
79	0	3	1	3	6	22860.	22580.	0.0917	-0.06
80	0	0	0	1	5	21980.	22560.	0.0917	-0.06
81	0	2	0	3	4	22020.	22450.	0.0917	-0.06
82	0	2	0	3	3	22500.	22190.	0.0917	-0.06
83	0	2	0	1	4	22860.	22270.	0.0917	-0.06
84	0	1	0	1	4	22690.	22330.	0.0917	-0.06
85	1	3	1	5	2	22770.	22760.	0.0917	-0.06
86	0	2	1	3	0	23160.	22990.	0.0958	-0.08
87	0	1	0	1	0	23560.	23140.	0.0958	-0.08
88	1	1	1	1	0	24880.	23480.	0.0958	-0.08
89	0	1	0	1	0	24660.	23710.	0.0958	-0.08
90	0	3	0	2	1	24600.	24080.	0.0958	-0.08
91	0	1	0	1	1	24400.	24130.	0.0958	-0.08
92	1	2	1	3	0	25150.	24940.	0.0958	-0.08
93	0	0	0	0	0	0.	24940.	0.0958	-0.08
94	1	4	1	1	4	25570.	25070.	0.0917	-0.06
95	0	2	1	1	4	25680.	25190.	0.0958	-0.05
96	1	3	0	3	5	25410.	25460.	0.0917	-0.06
97	0	3	0	1	7	24260.	25410.	0.0917	-0.06
98	0	2	0	2	7	26300.	25590.	0.0917	-0.06
99	1	4	0	3	9	25530.	25530.	0.0875	-0.03
100	0	6	0	2	13	24390.	25320.	0.0875	-0.03

CYCLE NUMBR	NEGRO LEAVE	WHITE LEAVE	NEGRO ENTER	WHITE ENTER	TOTAL VACNT	AVERG COST	PRIC AVERG	PROP NEGRO	SEGRE INDEX
101	1	3	2	2	13	25120.	25110.	0.0917	-0.06
102	0	1	0	4	10	25330.	25060.	0.0917	-0.06
103	0	4	0	2	12	26270.	25430.	0.0917	-0.06
104	0	0	0	1	11	24270.	25400.	0.0917	-0.06
105	1	0	0	4	8	23880.	24860.	0.0875	-0.03
106	0	2	0	3	7	24370.	24540.	0.0875	-0.03
107	0	1	0	0	8	0.	24540.	0.0875	-0.03
108	0	2	0	3	7	23310.	23860.	0.0875	-0.03
109	0	0	1	2	4	25130.	24130.	0.0917	-0.02
110	0	4	0	3	5	24410.	24150.	0.0917	-0.02
111	0	3	1	1	6	24610.	24420.	0.0958	-0.00
112	0	1	0	0	5	24360.	24580.	0.0958	-0.00
113	0	4	1	2	9	23660.	24530.	0.0958	-0.05
114	0	3	1	0	8	24530.	24330.	0.0958	-0.03
115	0	3	0	3	10	24770.	24340.	0.1000	-0.03
116	0	3	0	1	10	24100.	24240.	0.1000	-0.03
117	0	2	0	2	14	24160.	24300.	0.1000	-0.03
118	0	8	0	4	15	24900.	24440.	0.1000	-0.07
119	0	3	0	2	14	23810.	24190.	0.1000	-0.07
120	0	2	1	3	14	23590.	24120.	0.1042	-0.05
121	0	2	1	1	12	23900.	24040.	0.1083	-0.03
122	0	2	0	3	10	23080.	23600.	0.1083	-0.03
123	0	2	0	4	12	0.	23600.	0.1083	-0.03
124	1	4	0	2	15	23060.	23490.	0.1042	-0.01
125	0	1	1	3	12	23030.	23080.	0.1083	-0.03

CYCLE NUMBR	NEGRO LEAVE	WHITE LEAVE	NEGRO ENTER	WHITE ENTER	TOTAL VACNT	AVERG COST	PRIC AVERG	PROP NEGRO	SEGRE INDEX
126	0	4	1	0	15	22880.	23070.	0.1125	-0.05
127	0	3	0	3	15	22680.	22940.	0.1125	-0.05
128	0	1	1	2	13	22760.	22900.	0.1167	-0.07
129	0	1	0	3	11	22610.	22730.	0.1167	-0.07
130	0	4	1	2	12	22010.	22500.	0.1208	-0.02
131	1	5	0	5	13	22500.	22300.	0.1167	-0.04
132	1	2	0	10	6	22950.	22950.	0.1125	-0.05
133	0	3	0	1	8	22750.	22950.	0.1125	-0.05
134	1	2	0	4	7	22890.	22920.	0.1083	-0.07
135	1	2	2	2	6	23380.	23100.	0.1125	-0.09
136	0	4	0	1	9	23050.	23090.	0.1125	-0.09
137	0	2	0	2	9	23550.	23130.	0.1125	-0.09
138	0	0	0	2	7	23360.	23290.	0.1125	-0.09
139	0	1	0	2	6	22680.	23180.	0.1125	-0.09
140	0	3	0	3	6	22700.	23030.	0.1125	-0.09
141	0	1	0	3	4	23100.	22950.	0.1125	-0.09
142	0	3	0	2	5	23360.	22950.	0.1125	-0.09
143	0	2	1	2	4	23320.	23120.	0.1167	-0.07
144	1	1	1	2	3	24040.	23480.	0.1167	-0.07
145	0	2	0	3	2	23390.	23490.	0.1167	-0.07
146	1	2	0	0	5	0.	23490.	0.1125	-0.05
147	0	4	0	2	7	23570.	23540.	0.1125	-0.05
148	0	2	0	2	7	23340.	23530.	0.1125	-0.05
149	0	0	1	3	3	23590.	23500.	0.1167	-0.04
150	0	3	0	2	4.	24440.	23690.	0.1167	-0.04

Table 7. Invasion and Succession

PROBABILITY OF LEAVING   .01

NUMBER OF NEGROES SEEKING HOUSING   10

NUMBER OF WHITES SEEKING HOUSING   20

LEVEL OF ACQUISITIVENESS FOR BOTH   1

LEVEL OF PREJUDICE FOR WHITES   5

NEGRO PURCHASING POWER MEAN   10400

WHITE PURCHASING POWER MEAN   14760

CYCLE NUMBR	NEGRO LEAVE	WHITE LEAVE	NEGRO ENTER	WHITE ENTER	TOTAL VACNT	AVERG COST	PRIC AVERG	PROP NEGRO	SEGRE INDEX
1	0	1	0	1	0	15750.	15000.	0.0000	0.00
2	0	2	1	1	0	15820.	15070.	0.0042	0.00
3	1	6	1	2	4	16090.	15230.	0.0042	0.00
4	1	2	0	6	1	16090.	15530.	0.0000	0.00
5	0	3	0	3	1	16090.	16030.	0.0042	0.00
6	0	4	1	4	0	16710.	16080.	0.0000	0.00
7	1	1	0	0	2	0.	16510.	0.0000	0.00
8	0	1	1	0	3	16560.	16510.	0.0000	0.00
9	1	3	0	4	2	16650.	16650.	0.0000	0.00
10	0	1	0	1	2	16850.	16710.	0.0000	0.00
11	0	2	0	2	2	16950.	16700.	0.0000	0.00
12	0	0	0	2	0	0.	16780.	0.0000	0.00
13	0	0	0	0	0	17750.	16780.	0.0000	0.00
14	0	3	0	3	0	17920.	17070.	0.0000	0.00
15	0	2	0	2	1	17470.	17330.	0.0000	0.00
16	0	4	0	3	2	18370.	17540.	0.0000	0.00
17	0	4	2	1	7	18240.	17900.	0.0083	1.00
18	0	8	0	3	4	18090.	18050.	0.0083	1.00
19	0	1	0	4	3	18650.	18220.	0.0083	1.00
20	0	5	0	6	2	18650.	18430.	0.0083	1.00
21	0	2	0	3	4	0.	18630.	0.0083	1.00
22	0	2	0	0	4	19000.	18630.	0.0083	1.00
23	0	8	1	7	3	19290.	18890.	0.0125	-0.91
24	1	4	0	5	3	19290.	19210.	0.0125	-0.91
25	1	6	0	1	9	20170.	19340.	0.0083	-1.00

CYCLE NUMBR	NEGRO LEAVE	WHITE LEAVE	NEGRO ENTER	WHITE ENTER	TOTAL VACNT	AVERG COST	PRIC AVERG	PROP NEGRO	SEGRE INDEX
26	0	7	1	3	12	19130.	19240.	0.0125	-0.91
27	0	7	1	2	16	19780.	19450.	0.0167	-1.00
28	0	4	1	4	15	19110.	19320.	0.0208	-1.00
29	0	10	0	4	21	18690.	19010.	0.0208	-1.00
30	0	9	1	1	28	18800.	18950.	0.0250	-0.28
31	0	9	0	6	31	18800.	18890.	0.0250	-0.28
32	0	9	1	3	36	19050.	18950.	0.0292	-0.25
33	0	4	0	5	35	18470.	18800.	0.0292	-0.25
34	0	17	0	2	50	18190.	18660.	0.0292	-0.25
35	0	9	0	3	56	18070.	18290.	0.0292	-0.25
36	0	9	1	2	62	17700.	18120.	0.0333	-0.34
37	0	9	0	2	69	18530.	18100.	0.0333	-0.34
38	0	13	2	4	76	16910.	17500.	0.0417	-0.18
39	0	6	4	3	75	16920.	17040.	0.0583	-0.19
40	0	10	3	3	79	16920.	16990.	0.0708	-0.23
41	0	13	3	2	87	16700.	16910.	0.0833	-0.20
42	0	14	1	3	97	16620.	16650.	0.0875	-0.22
43	0	22	1	8	110	16110.	16310.	0.0917	-0.23
44	0	12	2	5	115	17460.	16980.	0.1000	-0.25
45	0	16	2	7	122	15840.	16140.	0.1083	-0.37
46	0	7	0	6	123	15920.	15970.	0.1083	-0.40
47	0	8	1	9	121	15520.	15790.	0.1125	-0.40
48	0	11	2	9	121	16980.	16510.	0.1208	-0.45
49	0	13	4	5	125	15770.	15880.	0.1375	-0.44
50	1	18	4	9	131	15770.	15730.	0.1500	-0.33

CYCLE NUMBR	NEGRO LEAVE	WHITE LEAVE	NEGRO ENTER	WHITE ENTER	TOTAL VACNT	AVERG COST	PRIC AVERG	PROP NEGRO	SEGRE INDEX
51	0	18	0	5	144	15030.	15310.	0.1500	-0.35
52	0	8	2	6	144	14270.	14390.	0.1583	-0.37
53	0	13	1	8	148	15870.	15000.	0.1625	-0.37
54	0	9	1	5	151	14420.	14910.	0.1667	-0.37
55	0	7	2	7	149	13850.	14070.	0.1750	-0.37
56	0	11	0	7	153	14060.	13960.	0.1750	-0.42
57	0	5	3	7	148	13670.	13680.	0.1875	-0.42
58	0	11	1	6	152	13100.	13410.	0.1917	-0.46
59	1	10	2	5	155	13910.	13330.	0.2000	-0.49
60	0	7	4	6	153	13510.	13680.	0.2125	-0.52
61	0	5	0	5	153	13350.	13640.	0.2125	-0.52
62	0	8	5	6	150	12750.	12860.	0.2333	-0.51
63	0	6	3	8	145	12210.	12290.	0.2458	-0.56
64	0	13	0	10	148	12680.	12680.	0.2458	-0.50
65	0	8	4	8	144	12410.	12770.	0.2625	-0.48
66	0	8	1	4	147	12530.	12830.	0.2667	-0.54
67	0	5	3	3	146	11740.	12300.	0.2792	-0.55
68	1	10	0	6	151	12000.	11880.	0.2750	-0.62
69	1	5	3	5	149	12220.	12210.	0.2833	-0.63
70	0	7	2	3	151	13160.	12950.	0.2917	-0.64
71	1	3	4	3	148	11120.	11730.	0.3042	-0.66
72	0	3	5	11	135	11430.	11210.	0.3250	-0.61
73	0	8	3	7	133	10920.	11020.	0.3375	-0.61
74	1	8	4	5	133	10440.	10530.	0.3500	-0.64
75	0	6	4	9	126	10830.	11230.	0.3667	-0.62

CYCLE NUMBR	NEGRO LEAVE	WHITE LEAVE	NEGRO ENTER	WHITE ENTER	TOTAL VACNT	AVERG COST	PRIC AVERG	PROP NEGRO	SEGRE INDEX
76	0	10	1	5	130	10620.	11070.	0.3708	-0.69
77	0	8	3	8	127	10650.	10910.	0.3833	-0.70
78	0	7	2	1	131	10370.	10760.	0.3917	-0.72
79	1	2	6	3	125	10880.	10920.	0.4125	-0.73
80	1	3	3	4	122	10390.	10420.	0.4208	-0.71
81	1	5	4	3	121	10260.	10280.	0.4333	-0.72
82	0	2	4	4	115	10450.	10460.	0.4500	-0.70
83	2	5	2	3	117	10480.	10460.	0.4500	-0.72
84	1	1	5	5	109	9960.	9960.	0.4667	-0.70
85	1	4	4	5	105	10200.	10320.	0.4792	-0.68
86	1	7	3	2	108	9400.	9630.	0.4875	-0.73
87	2	1	3	2	106	10040.	9690.	0.4917	-0.72
88	4	4	2	6	106	9630.	10040.	0.4833	-0.72
89	1	5	5	0	107	9420.	9700.	0.5000	-0.73
90	3	1	3	1	107	9520.	9430.	0.5000	-0.74
91	0	3	7	1	100	9190.	9400.	0.5292	-0.72
92	3	3	5	2	99	9590.	9410.	0.5375	-0.75
93	2	2	5	2	96	9110.	9140.	0.5500	-0.75
94	2	3	3	2	94	10110.	9640.	0.5542	-0.72
95	0	1	1	0	96	9340.	9660.	0.5583	-0.75
96	3	3	4	2	94	8870.	9180.	0.5625	-0.74
97	2	1	4	2	90	9110.	8970.	0.5708	-0.72
98	1	0	5	2	85	8910.	8890.	0.5875	-0.72
99	2	1	3	0	85	8770.	8810.	0.5917	-0.74
100	2	1	2	0	86	8740.	8840.	0.5917	-0.75

CYCLE NUMBR	NEGRO LEAVE	WHITE LEAVE	NEGRO ENTER	WHITE ENTER	TOTAL VACNT	AVERG COST	PRIC AVERG	PROP NEGRO	SEGRE INDEX
101	2	1	6	1	82	8800.	8630.	0.6083	-0.75
102	1	0	4	1	78	9200.	8920.	0.6208	-0.75
103	1	1	5	0	75	8310.	8730.	0.6375	-0.73
104	0	0	1	1	73	8540.	8490.	0.6417	-0.72
105	1	1	3	0	72	8530.	8420.	0.6500	-0.72
106	2	2	3	2	71	8690.	8620.	0.6542	-0.73
107	2	1	3	0	71	8500.	8630.	0.6583	-0.73
108	1	0	1	0	71	8520.	8650.	0.6583	-0.73
109	0	2	3	2	68	7970.	8220.	0.6708	-0.72
110	2	0	4	2	64	8370.	8200.	0.6792	-0.71
111	0	1	1	1	63	7840.	8190.	0.6833	-0.72
112	0	4	3	0	64	8170.	8180.	0.6958	-0.74
113	2	0	2	1	63	8100.	8100.	0.6958	-0.72
114	0	1	3	0	61	8160.	8090.	0.7083	-0.73
115	2	1	2	0	62	7590.	7990.	0.7083	-0.73
116	2	0	5	0	59	8000.	7960.	0.7208	-0.73
117	0	0	3	0	56	8150.	7960.	0.7333	-0.72
118	3	0	5	0	54	7880.	7890.	0.7417	-0.71
119	1	0	2	0	53	7330.	7850.	0.7458	-0.71
120	0	0	3	0	50	7500.	7660.	0.7583	-0.70
121	3	0	1	0	52	6990.	7560.	0.7500	-0.71
122	2	0	4	0	50	7510.	7420.	0.7583	-0.70
123	1	0	2	0	49	6990.	7350.	0.7625	-0.70
124	2	0	3	0	48	7230.	7270.	0.7667	-0.69
125	3	2	1	1	51	7070.	7310.	0.7583	-0.69

CYCLE NUMBR	NEGRO LEAVE	WHITE LEAVE	NEGRO ENTER	WHITE ENTER	TOTAL VACNT	AVERG COST	PRIC AVERG	PROP NEGRO	SEGRE INDEX
126	0	1	2	0	50	6790.	7150.	0.7667	-0.71
127	0	0	4	0	46	6850.	6930.	0.7833	-0.70
128	3	0	4	1	44	7050.	6870.	0.7875	-0.67
129	2	1	2	0	45	6680.	6830.	0.7875	-0.69
130	2	0	3	0	44	6630.	6780.	0.7917	-0.69
131	2	0	1	0	45	7270.	6820.	0.7875	-0.69
132	1	0	4	0	42	6400.	6610.	0.8000	-0.68
133	2	0	2	0	42	6690.	6610.	0.8000	-0.68
134	0	0	1	1	40	6030.	6510.	0.8042	-0.66
135	2	0	1	1	40	6480.	6400.	0.8000	-0.64
136	1	0	1	0	40	6000.	6350.	0.8000	-0.64
137	1	1	1	0	41	5890.	6320.	0.8000	-0.66
138	0	0	3	0	38	6010.	6220.	0.8125	-0.64
139	1	1	3	1	36	6240.	6130.	0.8208	-0.65
140	2	2	2	0	38	6200.	6140.	0.8208	-0.69
141	1	0	5	0	34	5970.	6150.	0.8375	-0.67
142	1	1	3	0	33	6150.	6070.	0.8458	-0.67
143	3	0	1	0	35	5920.	6000.	0.8375	-0.68
144	4	0	2	0	37	6060.	6030.	0.8292	-0.69
145	1	0	0	0	38	0.	6030.	0.8250	-0.69
146	5	0	0	0	43	0.	6030.	0.8042	-0.69
147	0	0	3	0	40	5530.	5910.	0.8167	-0.71
148	1	0	1	0	40	6210.	5930.	0.8167	-0.70
149	1	0	3	0	38	5690.	5790.	0.8250	-0.69
150	2	0	1	0	39	5500.	5750.	0.8208	-0.70

Table 8. A White Reservation

PROBABILITY OF LEAVING	.01
NUMBER OF NEGROES SEEKING HOUSING	10
NUMBER OF WHITES SEEKING HOUSING	20
LEVEL OF ACQUISITIVENESS FOR BOTH	1
LEVEL OF PREJUDICE FOR WHITES	7
NEGRO PURCHASING POWER MEAN	10400
WHITE PURCHASING POWER MEAN	14760

CYCLE NUMBR	NEGRO LEAVE	WHITE LEAVE	NEGRO ENTER	WHITE ENTER	TOTAL VACNT	NEGRO AVCOS	PRIC AVERG	PROP NEGRO	SEGRE INDEX
1	0	2	0	2	0	0.	15000.	0.0000	0.00
2	0	3	0	3	0	0.	15180.	0.0000	0.00
3	0	1	0	1	0	0.	15460.	0.0000	0.00
4	0	3	0	2	1	0.	15550.	0.0000	0.00
5	0	5	0	5	1	0.	15820.	0.0000	0.00
6	0	2	0	3	0	0.	16100.	0.0000	0.00
7	0	1	0	1	0	0.	16360.	0.0000	0.00
8	0	3	0	3	0	0.	16520.	0.0000	0.00
9	0	3	0	3	0	0.	16890.	0.0000	0.00
10	0	2	0	2	2	0.	17310.	0.0000	0.00
11	0	4	0	2	4	0.	17770.	0.0000	0.00
12	0	3	0	1	4	0.	17880.	0.0000	0.00
13	0	1	0	1	3	0.	17980.	0.0000	0.00
14	0	1	0	2	3	0.	18030.	0.0000	0.00
15	0	1	0	1	3	0.	18160.	0.0000	0.00
16	0	2	0	3	2	0.	18150.	0.0000	0.00
17	0	1	0	2	1	0.	18060.	0.0000	0.00
18	0	0	0	1	0	0.	18060.	0.0000	0.00
19	0	1	0	1	0	0.	18120.	0.0000	0.00
20	0	2	0	2	0	0.	18290.	0.0000	0.00
21	0	0	0	0	2	0.	18290.	0.0000	0.00
22	0	5	0	3	2	0.	18610.	0.0000	0.00
23	0	4	0	1	5	0.	18650.	0.0000	0.00
24	0	2	0	2	5	0.	18710.	0.0000	0.00
25	0	1	0	4	2	0.	18780.	0.0000	0.00

CYCLE NUMBR	NEGRO LEAVE	WHITE LEAVE	NEGRO ENTER	WHITE ENTER	TOTAL VACNT	NEGRO AVCOS	PRIC AVERG	PROP NEGRO	SEGRE INDEX
26	0	1	0	3	0	0.	18890.	0.0000	0.00
27	0	2	0	2	0	0.	19100.	0.0000	0.00
28	0	5	0	1	4	0.	19160.	0.0000	0.00
29	0	3	0	5	2	0.	19660.	0.0000	0.00
30	0	2	0	2	2	0.	19700.	0.0000	0.00
31	0	1	0	2	1	0.	19770.	0.0000	0.00
32	0	6	0	3	4	0.	20000.	0.0000	0.00
33	0	3	0	3	4	0.	20120.	0.0000	0.00
34	0	4	0	3	5	0.	20240.	0.0000	0.00
35	0	3	0	1	7	0.	20250.	0.0000	0.00
36	0	2	0	3	6	0.	20190.	0.0000	0.00
37	0	2	0	2	6	0.	20120.	0.0000	0.00
38	0	1	0	4	3	0.	20120.	0.0000	0.00
39	0	0	0	2	1	0.	20140.	0.0000	0.00
40	0	2	0	2	1	0.	20230.	0.0000	0.00
41	0	2	0	2	2	0.	20340.	0.0000	0.00
42	0	1	0	1	2	0.	20490.	0.0000	0.00
43	0	3	0	1	1	0.	20820.	0.0000	0.00
44	0	2	0	4	0	0.	21240.	0.0000	0.00
45	0	1	0	3	0	0.	21360.	0.0000	0.00
46	0	0	0	1	0	0.	21360.	0.0000	0.00
47	0	2	0	0	1	0.	21480.	0.0000	0.00
48	0	1	0	1	1	0.	21540.	0.0000	0.00
49	0	4	0	4	1	0.	22110.	0.0000	0.00
50	0	4	0	2	3	0.	22330.	0.0000	0.00

CYCLE NUMBR	NEGRO LEAVE	WHITE LEAVE	NEGRO ENTER	WHITE ENTER	TOTAL VACNT	NEGRO AVCOS	PRIC AVERG	PROP NEGRO	SEGRE INDEX
51	0	4	0	0	7	0.	22330.	0.0000	0.00
52	0	1	0	2	6	0.	22320.	0.0000	0.00
53	0	2	0	6	2	0.	22390.	0.0000	0.00
54	0	2	0	2	2	0.	22490.	0.0000	0.00
55	0	1	0	3	0	0.	22800.	0.0000	0.00
56	0	2	0	2	0	0.	23160.	0.0000	0.00
57	0	1	0	0	1	0.	23160.	0.0000	0.00
58	0	2	0	1	2	0.	23290.	0.0000	0.00
59	0	4	0	2	4	0.	23600.	0.0000	0.00
60	0	1	0	2	3	0.	23730.	0.0000	0.00
61	0	3	0	5	1	0.	23840.	0.0000	0.00
62	0	2	0	2	1	0.	24020.	0.0000	0.00
63	0	2	0	3	0	0.	24280.	0.0000	0.00
64	0	2	0	1	1	0.	24380.	0.0000	0.00
65	0	3	0	1	3	0.	24790.	0.0000	0.00
66	0	3	0	3	3	0.	25290.	0.0000	0.00
67	0	2	0	4	1	0.	25260.	0.0000	0.00
68	0	0	0	1	0	0.	25360.	0.0000	0.00
69	0	3	0	1	2	0.	25520.	0.0000	0.00
70	0	6	0	2	6	0.	25520.	0.0000	0.00
71	0	2	0	0	8	0.	25520.	0.0000	0.00
72	0	7	0	0	15	0.	25540.	0.0000	0.00
73	0	1	0	4	12	0.	25540.	0.0000	0.00
74	0	2	0	2	12	0.	25150.	0.0000	0.00
75	0	1	0	3	10	0.	24950.	0.0000	0.00

CYCLE NUMBR	NEGRO LEAVE	WHITE LEAVE	NEGRO ENTER	WHITE ENTER	TOTAL VACNT	NEGRO AVCOS	PRIC AVERG	PROP NEGRO	SEGRE INDEX
76	0	4	0	2	12	0.	24600.	0.0000	0.00
77	0	2	0	0	14	0.	24600.	0.0000	0.00
78	0	4	0	1	17	0.	24530.	0.0000	0.00
79	0	2	0	3	16	0.	24260.	0.0000	0.00
80	0	1	0	3	14	0.	24030.	0.0000	0.00
81	0	2	0	1	15	0.	23920.	0.0000	0.00
82	0	1	0	3	13	0.	23810.	0.0000	0.00
83	0	4	0	2	15	0.	23810.	0.0000	0.00
84	0	2	0	2	15	0.	23450.	0.0000	0.00
85	0	1	0	1	15	0.	23280.	0.0000	0.00
86	0	2	0	4	13	0.	22760.	0.0000	0.00
87	0	1	0	1	13	0.	22830.	0.0000	0.00
88	0	2	0	2	13	0.	22600.	0.0000	0.00
89	0	2	0	1	14	0.	22730.	0.0000	0.00
90	0	4	0	2	16	0.	22880.	0.0000	0.00
91	0	0	0	3	13	0.	22550.	0.0000	0.00
92	0	1	0	2	12	0.	22220.	0.0000	0.00
93	0	0	0	2	10	0.	22090.	0.0000	0.00
94	0	2	0	1	11	0.	21840.	0.0000	0.00
95	0	3	0	4	10	0.	21500.	0.0000	0.00
96	0	0	0	3	7	0.	21530.	0.0000	0.00
97	0	6	0	2	11	0.	21700.	0.0000	0.00
98	0	2	0	5	8	0.	21830.	0.0000	0.00
99	0	0	0	0	8	0.	21830.	0.0000	0.00
100	0	1	0	4	5	0.	21420.	0.0000	0.00

CYCLE NUMBR	NEGRO LEAVE	WHITE LEAVE	NEGRO ENTER	WHITE ENTER	TOTAL VACNT	NEGRO AVCOS	PRIC AVERG	PROP NEGRO	SEGRE INDEX
101	0	1	0	4	2	0.	21380.	0.0000	0.00
102	0	1	0	2	1	0.	21470.	0.0000	0.00
103	0	2	0	2	1	0.	21670.	0.0000	0.00
104	0	3	0	3	1	0.	21980.	0.0000	0.00
105	0	3	0	3	1	0.	22320.	0.0000	0.00
106	0	1	0	1	1	0.	22380.	0.0000	0.00
107	0	1	0	2	0	0.	22510.	0.0000	0.00
108	0	4	0	0	4	0.	22510.	0.0000	0.00
109	0	1	0	1	4	0.	22570.	0.0000	0.00
110	0	2	0	1	5	0.	22620.	0.0000	0.00
111	0	0	0	2	3	0.	22570.	0.0000	0.00
112	0	5	0	2	6	0.	22610.	0.0000	0.00
113	0	2	0	3	5	0.	22630.	0.0000	0.00
114	0	6	0	7	4	0.	22990.	0.0000	0.00
115	0	2	0	5	1	0.	23470.	0.0000	0.00
116	0	5	0	0	6	0.	23470.	0.0000	0.00
117	0	2	0	3	5	0.	23790.	0.0000	0.00
118	0	3	0	2	6	0.	23750.	0.0000	0.00
119	0	5	0	2	9	0.	23960.	0.0000	0.00
120	0	5	0	4	10	0.	23980.	0.0000	0.00
121	0	1	0	1	10	0.	23970.	0.0000	0.00
122	0	1	0	6	5	0.	23580.	0.0000	0.00
123	0	0	0	3	2	0.	23230.	0.0000	0.00
124	0	3	0	1	4	0.	23290.	0.0000	0.00
125	0	2	0	4	2	0.	23560.	0.0000	0.00

CYCLE NUMBR	NEGRO LEAVE	WHITE LEAVE	NEGRO ENTER	WHITE ENTER	TOTAL VACNT	NEGRO AVCOS	PRIC AVERG	PROP NEGRO	SEGRE INDEX
126	0	5	0	3	4	0.	23690.	0.0000	0.00
127	0	1	0	3	2	0.	23810.	0.0000	0.00
128	0	3	0	1	4	0.	23860.	0.0000	0.00
129	0	3	0	3	4	0.	23870.	0.0000	0.00
130	0	2	0	1	5	0.	23900.	0.0000	0.00
131	0	2	0	5	2	0.	24050.	0.0000	0.00
132	0	3	0	1	4	0.	24140.	0.0000	0.00
133	0	2	0	1	5	0.	24230.	0.0000	0.00
134	0	1	0	3	3	0.	24280.	0.0000	0.00
135	0	6	0	1	8	0.	24430.	0.0000	0.00
136	0	3	0	3	8	0.	24350.	0.0000	0.00
137	0	4	0	1	11	0.	24440.	0.0000	0.00
138	0	2	0	4	9	0.	24210.	0.0000	0.00
139	0	2	0	3	8	0.	24070.	0.0000	0.00
140	0	3	0	4	7	0.	24040.	0.0000	0.00
141	0	2	0	1	8	0.	24080.	0.0000	0.00
142	0	3	0	4	7	0.	24030.	0.0000	0.00
143	0	2	0	2	7	0.	23950.	0.0000	0.00
144	0	5	0	1	11	0.	23840.	0.0000	0.00
145	0	2	0	1	12	0.	23740.	0.0000	0.00
146	0	4	0	3	13	0.	23660.	0.0000	0.00
147	0	5	0	3	15	0.	23430.	0.0000	0.00
148	0	0	0	4	11	0.	23310.	0.0000	0.00
149	0	4	0	2	13	0.	23390.	0.0000	0.00
150	0	2	0	1	14	0.	23160.	0.0000	0.00

Table 9. An Interethnic Neighborhood, I

PROBABILITY OF LEAVING	.01
NUMBER OF NEGROES SEEKING HOUSING	10
NUMBER OF WHITES SEEKING HOUSING	20
LEVEL OF ACQUISITIVENESS FOR BOTH	1
LEVEL OF PREJUDICE FOR WHITES	2
NEGRO PURCHASING POWER MEAN	10400
WHITE PURCHASING POWER MEAN	14760

CYCLE NUMBR	NEGRO LEAVE	WHITE LEAVE	NEGRO ENTER	WHITE ENTER	TOTAL VACNT	AVERG COST	PRIC AVERG	PROP NEGRO	SEGRE INDEX
1	0	3	2	1	0	15930.	15000.	0.0083	1.00
2	1	1	0	2	0	16400.	15260.	0.0042	1.00
3	1	6	2	3	2	16310.	15540.	0.0083	1.00
4	1	4	2	4	1	16640.	16190.	0.0125	1.00
5	0	4	2	1	2	17140.	16520.	0.0208	1.00
6	0	4	1	2	3	17220.	16780.	0.0250	1.00
7	0	8	3	2	6	17320.	16910.	0.0375	-0.07
8	0	7	0	2	11	17390.	17270.	0.0375	-0.07
9	0	5	1	5	10	17310.	17280.	0.0417	-0.05
10	0	2	0	3	9	17100.	17470.	0.0417	-0.05
11	0	8	0	7	11	17640.	17390.	0.0375	-0.07
12	1	6	1	3	13	17510.	17480.	0.0417	-0.18
13	0	9	1	1	20	17130.	17440.	0.0458	-0.14
14	0	7	1	2	24	17640.	17530.	0.0500	-0.10
15	0	7	2	4	28	18050.	17760.	0.0542	-0.15
16	0	8	0	6	31	16860.	17410.	0.0583	-0.14
17	1	6	1	2	31	16760.	16740.	0.0583	-0.14
18	0	9	1	3	38	16820.	16820.	0.0583	-0.19
19	1	10	0	2	44	16110.	16590.	0.0625	-0.18
20	0	9	2	5	50	16310.	16390.	0.0667	-0.21
21	0	10	1	3	56	16310.	16250.	0.0625	-0.25
22	1	7	0	5	58	16270.	16320.	0.0708	-0.23
23	0	6	2	4	58	15770.	16070.	0.0750	-0.19
24	0	9	1	6	62	15670.	15810.	0.0792	-0.26
25	1	4	1		60	16570.	16090.	0.0792	-0.17

CYCLE NUMBR	NEGRO LEAVE	WHITE LEAVE	NEGRO ENTER	WHITE ENTER	TOTAL VACNT	AVERG COST	PRIC AVERG	PROP NEGRO	SEGRE INDEX
26	0	11	1	5	65	15690.	16260.	0.0833	-0.20
27	0	3	1	6	61	15020.	15250.	0.0875	-0.22
28	0	10	2	4	65	15460.	15260.	0.0958	-0.24
29	0	7	0	1	71	15470.	15310.	0.0958	-0.24
30	2	12	2	6	75	14750.	15050.	0.1042	-0.29
31	2	4	0	5	76	14190.	14570.	0.0958	-0.28
32	0	9	3	5	77	14410.	14390.	0.1083	-0.33
33	0	10	2	4	81	14200.	14270.	0.1167	-0.37
34	1	6	3	7	78	14240.	14210.	0.1250	-0.33
35	0	4	1	5	76	14120.	14260.	0.1292	-0.27
36	0	6	0	6	76	14140.	14180.	0.1292	-0.24
37	0	4	2	4	74	13520.	13700.	0.1375	-0.21
38	0	8	1	5	76	13690.	13700.	0.1417	-0.22
39	1	6	1	6	76	13450.	13580.	0.1417	-0.19
40	0	4	3	6	71	13620.	13790.	0.1542	-0.20
41	0	8	2	5	72	13450.	13600.	0.1625	-0.23
42	2	7	2	5	74	13410.	13430.	0.1625	-0.19
43	0	5	2	6	71	13390.	13400.	0.1708	-0.16
44	2	7	2	3	75	13190.	13300.	0.1708	-0.18
45	0	7	1	8	73	13480.	13250.	0.1750	-0.16
46	0	7	2	9	69	12920.	13000.	0.1833	-0.16
47	0	9	3	7	68	13270.	13320.	0.1958	-0.19
48	0	6	4	6	64	12950.	12940.	0.2125	-0.20
49	1	10	2	8	65	12620.	12710.	0.2167	-0.20
50	0	7	4	8	60	12740.	12800.	0.2333	-0.22

CYCLE NUMBR	NEGRO LEAVE	WHITE LEAVE	NEGRO ENTER	WHITE ENTER	TOTAL VACNT	AVERG COST	PRIC AVERG	PROP NEGRO	SEGRE INDEX
51	1	11	2	8	62	12600.	12650.	0.2375	-0.22
52	0	8	2	4	64	12330.	12580.	0.2458	-0.22
53	0	7	2	6	63	12150.	12210.	0.2542	-0.17
54	0	9	1	6	65	12140.	12230.	0.2583	-0.19
55	0	7	2	6	64	12280.	12310.	0.2667	-0.19
56	1	3	0	3	65	12160.	12280.	0.2625	-0.18
57	0	3	1	7	60	11690.	11760.	0.2667	-0.17
58	0	12	3	5	64	11550.	11600.	0.2792	-0.16
59	1	8	1	5	67	11690.	11830.	0.2792	-0.17
60	0	7	4	5	65	11890.	11870.	0.2958	-0.16
61	0	5	3	3	64	11520.	11770.	0.3083	-0.15
62	0	5	4	7	58	11350.	11210.	0.3250	-0.15
63	0	7	1	4	60	11060.	11160.	0.3292	-0.17
64	0	5	2	4	59	10990.	11050.	0.3375	-0.17
65	1	7	4	3	60	11260.	11180.	0.3500	-0.18
66	0	5	2	6	57	11570.	11380.	0.3583	-0.19
67	1	10	2	8	58	11470.	11370.	0.3625	-0.19
68	1	4	3	5	55	11330.	11370.	0.3708	-0.19
69	1	8	4	5	55	10820.	10810.	0.3833	-0.20
70	0	6	1	5	55	11200.	10890.	0.3875	-0.22
71	0	4	0	7	52	10590.	10600.	0.3875	-0.21
72	1	7	5	7	48	10620.	10630.	0.4042	-0.21
73	1	12	3	6	52	10430.	10590.	0.4125	-0.22
74	1	7	4	4	52	10590.	10530.	0.4250	-0.20
75	0	6	2	7	49	10230.	10290.	0.4333	-0.18

CYCLE NUMBR	NEGRO LEAVE	WHITE LEAVE	NEGRO ENTER	WHITE ENTER	TOTAL VACNT	AVERG COST	PRIC AVERG	PROP NEGRO	SEGRE INDEX
76	0	3	2	4	46	10450.	10330.	0.4417	-0.19
77	1	4	1	4	46	9880.	10190.	0.4417	-0.18
78	2	1	4	3	42	10030.	9980.	0.4500	-0.16
79	1	4	2	6	39	9810.	9940.	0.4542	-0.17
80	1	4	2	5	37	9980.	9840.	0.4583	-0.16
81	3	2	3	2	37	9780.	9740.	0.4583	-0.14
82	1	7	3	3	39	9770.	9810.	0.4667	-0.10
83	1	7	5	6	36	9930.	9850.	0.4833	-0.12
84	1	4	3	3	35	9580.	9760.	0.4917	-0.15
85	0	3	2	4	32	9700.	9610.	0.5000	-0.15
86	0	3	3	3	29	9690.	9630.	0.5125	-0.13
87	0	2	2	7	22	9850.	9740.	0.5208	-0.12
88	2	4	2	3	23	9420.	9520.	0.5208	-0.10
89	0	6	3	2	24	9490.	9460.	0.5333	-0.10
90	0	6	3	7	20	9430.	9420.	0.5458	-0.06
91	1	4	1	2	22	9310.	9310.	0.5458	-0.04
92	2	4	3	5	20	9120.	9140.	0.5500	-0.06
93	0	5	1	5	19	9470.	9420.	0.5542	-0.05
94	3	5	3	5	18	9250.	9260.	0.5542	-0.01
95	1	4	3	3	17	9250.	9240.	0.5625	0.02
96	2	3	3	1	18	9330.	9220.	0.5667	0.02
97	1	7	3	2	21	9080.	9270.	0.5750	-0.01
98	0	1	1	0	21	9060.	0260.	0.5792	-0.01
99	4	1	4	1	21	9000.	9190.	0.5792	-0.03
100	1	4	5	4	17		9010.	0.5958	-0.01

CYCLE NUMBR	NEGRO LEAVE	WHITE LEAVE	NEGRO ENTER	WHITE ENTER	TOTAL VACNT	AVERG COST	PRIC AVERG	PROP NEGRO	SEGRE INDEX
101	0	2	4	1	14	8870.	8910.	0.6125	0.00
102	1	5	3	2	15	9130.	8960.	0.6208	-0.02
103	3	1	1	3	15	9020.	9080.	0.6125	-0.06
104	2	4	4	1	16	9010.	9040.	0.6208	-0.06
105	2	2	2	3	15	8930.	9000.	0.6208	-0.05
106	2	3	1	5	14	9340.	9080.	0.6167	-0.02
107	0	5	2	1	16	8730.	8970.	0.6250	-0.06
108	2	2	4	1	15	8980.	9040.	0.6333	-0.07
109	1	2	3	2	13	8820.	8910.	0.6417	-0.06
110	2	3	2	5	11	9000.	8980.	0.6417	-0.04
111	1	2	3	4	7	9040.	9090.	0.6500	-0.02
112	1	3	2	2	7	9200.	9130.	0.6542	-0.03
113	1	0	0	4	4	9140.	9160.	0.6500	-0.01
114	2	1	1	0	6	8860.	9130.	0.6458	-0.04
115	1	4	3	2	6	9400.	9220.	0.6542	-0.06
116	4	0	4	1	5	9350.	9340.	0.6542	-0.03
117	0	3	2	2	4	9460.	9370.	0.6625	-0.01
118	1	2	2	0	5	9290.	9380.	0.6667	-0.00
119	2	1	3	3	2	9520.	9500.	0.6708	-0.02
120	3	3	1	1	6	9750.	9520.	0.6625	-0.01
121	2	2	0	4	6	9690.	9690.	0.6542	-0.01
122	1	1	4	2	2	9890.	9810.	0.6667	-0.01
123	5	5	3	4	5	10040.	10050.	0.6583	-0.00
124	0	2	1	0	6	9950.	10080.	0.6625	-0.00
125	1	1	2	1	5	9850.	9940.	0.6667	-0.00

CYCLE NUMBR	NEGRO LEAVE	WHITE LEAVE	NEGRO ENTER	WHITE ENTER	TOTAL VACNT	AVERG COST	PRIC AVERG	PROP NEGRO	SEGRE INDEX
126	0	0	2	3	0	10100.	10000.	0.6750	0.01
127	2	1	3	0	0	10500.	10190.	0.6792	0.01
128	3	1	2	2	0	10440.	10370.	0.6750	0.00
129	1	2	0	2	1	11150.	10570.	0.6708	-0.01
130	1	0	2	2	0	10750.	10680.	0.6750	-0.00
131	0	4	2	1	0	11210.	10980.	0.6833	-0.03
132	2	1	1	2	1	11520.	11170.	0.6792	-0.04
133	2	1	1	2	1	11580.	11360.	0.6750	-0.03
134	2	3	2	2	2	11810.	11660.	0.6750	-0.00
135	3	0	3	2	0	12010.	11920.	0.6750	-0.00
136	0	1	0	1	0	11920.	11910.	0.6750	-0.00
137	2	0	1	1	0	12210.	12010.	0.6708	-0.00
138	2	0	1	0	0	12760.	12180.	0.6667	-0.00
139	2	1	0	0	3	0.	12180.	0.6583	-0.04
140	0	1	3	1	1	12580.	12350.	0.6708	-0.02
141	3	1	1	3	3	12900.	12540.	0.6625	-0.04
142	1	2	2	1	1	12580.	12630.	0.6667	-0.00
143	2	4	2	4	4	13210.	12820.	0.6667	-0.01
144	2	0	0	1	0	13190.	13160.	0.6667	0.01
145	0	3	2	0	2	13490.	13260.	0.6667	-0.01
146	5	0	2	2	5	13260.	13280.	0.6542	-0.03
147	4	0	2	1	5	13600.	13490.	0.6458	-0.02
148	1	2	2	1	5	13570.	13500.	0.6500	-0.01
149	0	1	2	2	2	13960.	13760.	0.6583	0.00
150	4	2	2	5	1	14130.	14040.	0.6500	0.00

Table 10. An Interethnic Neighborhood, II

PROBABILITY OF LEAVING	.01
NUMBER OF NEGROES SEEKING HOUSING	10
NUMBER OF WHITES SEEKING HOUSING	20
LEVEL OF ACQUISITIVENESS FOR BOTH	1
LEVEL OF PREJUDICE FOR WHITES	2
NEGRO PURCHASING POWER MEAN	14760
WHITE PURCHASING POWER MEAN	14760

CYCLE NUMBR	NEGRO LEAVE	WHITE LEAVE	NEGRO ENTER	WHITE ENTER	TOTAL VACNT	AVERG COST	PRIC AVERG	PROP NEGRO	SEGRE INDEX
1	0	4	1	3	0	15620.	15000.	0.0042	0.00
2	0	3	2	1	0	15680.	15290.	0.0125	-0.91
3	1	3	1	3	0	16590.	15500.	0.0125	1.00
4	0	4	1	3	0	16740.	16010.	0.0167	1.00
5	0	1	0	1	0	17590.	16360.	0.0167	1.00
6	1	3	0	4	0	17480.	16550.	0.0125	1.00
7	0	3	1	2	0	18010.	17060.	0.0167	1.00
8	0	5	2	3	0	18370.	17570.	0.0250	1.00
9	0	5	1	3	1	19360.	18150.	0.0292	1.00
10	0	6	3	3	1	19530.	18720.	0.0417	-0.05
11	0	7	2	4	2	20650.	19430.	0.0500	-0.10
12	0	10	3	3	6	20810.	20210.	0.0625	-0.18
13	0	10	3	1	12	20860.	20740.	0.0750	-0.19
14	0	10	2	1	19	20570.	20850.	0.0833	-0.24
15	0	10	1	2	26	21020.	20910.	0.0875	-0.26
16	1	6	1	1	31	20820.	20780.	0.0875	-0.26
17	0	12	2	3	38	20280.	20740.	0.0958	-0.20
18	0	10	1	3	44	20440.	20590.	0.1000	-0.21
19	0	14	3	2	53	20300.	20330.	0.1125	-0.25
20	0	7	2	4	54	18830.	20140.	0.1208	-0.23
21	0	7	1	7	53	18800.	19440.	0.1250	-0.24
22	0	13	2	2	62	19000.	18960.	0.1333	-0.28
23	0	9	0	5	66	19030.	19010.	0.1333	-0.28
24	0	8	1	8	65	18540.	19060.	0.1375	-0.30
25	0	8	2	5	66	18490.	18510.	0.1458	-0.30

CYCLE NUMBR	NEGRO LEAVE	WHITE LEAVE	NEGRO ENTER	WHITE ENTER	TOTAL VACNT	AVERG COST	PRIC AVERG	PROP NEGRO	SEGRE INDEX
26	1	7	4	1	69	18070.	18340.	0.1583	-0.25
27	0	12	3	3	75	18480.	18380.	0.1708	-0.19
28	1	6	3	2	77	18250.	18390.	0.1792	-0.16
29	2	12	2	8	81	17710.	17820.	0.1792	-0.20
30	0	9	3	5	82	17460.	17690.	0.1917	-0.21
31	0	3	2	7	76	18020.	17630.	0.2000	-0.21
32	1	12	5	3	81	17660.	17380.	0.2167	-0.19
33	1	8	1	3	86	16630.	17380.	0.2167	-0.19
34	0	5	0	6	85	16510.	16610.	0.2167	-0.18
35	0	10	3	6	86	16570.	16640.	0.2292	-0.19
36	1	5	1	3	88	17990.	16850.	0.2292	-0.22
37	1	4	3	4	86	16060.	16320.	0.2375	-0.25
38	0	6	4	5	83	16100.	16100.	0.2542	-0.23
39	0	1	1	6	77	16360.	16700.	0.2583	-0.21
40	0	5	3	6	73	16620.	16560.	0.2708	-0.19
41	3	11	4	9	74	15980.	16000.	0.2750	-0.12
42	1	6	2	8	71	15730.	15500.	0.2792	-0.08
43	0	11	2	5	75	15150.	15210.	0.2875	-0.09
44	0	4	2	8	69	15150.	15330.	0.2958	-0.11
45	2	3	3	7	64	15290.	15450.	0.3000	-0.09
46	0	8	2	3	67	15010.	15410.	0.3083	-0.12
47	1	4	0	4	68	15200.	15120.	0.3042	-0.14
48	1	7	3	5	68	14690.	14940.	0.3125	-0.15
49	0	5	1	5	67	14580.	14850.	0.3167	-0.13
50	1	7	3	5	67	14610.	14760.	0.3250	-0.13

CYCLE NUMBR	NEGRO LEAVE	WHITE LEAVE	NEGRO ENTER	WHITE ENTER	TOTAL VACNT	AVERG COST	PRIC AVERG	PROP NEGRO	SEGRE INDEX
51	0	5	3	3	66	14920.	14910.	0.3375	-0.13
52	1	9	3	9	64	14410.	14460.	0.3458	-0.15
53	0	7	4	5	62	15070.	15040.	0.3625	-0.19
54	0	6	2	2	64	14310.	14640.	0.3708	-0.22
55	1	9	1	5	68	14540.	14450.	0.3708	-0.20
56	2	3	3	8	62	14090.	14160.	0.3750	-0.15
57	2	6	4	3	63	13960.	14040.	0.3833	-0.19
58	0	6	3	4	62	13760.	13940.	0.3958	-0.18
59	0	4	2	4	60	13740.	13720.	0.4042	-0.20
60	0	7	2	4	61	13870.	13750.	0.4125	-0.23
61	0	4	4	5	56	13550.	13700.	0.4292	-0.21
62	1	7	4	7	53	13580.	13720.	0.4417	-0.21
63	1	3	3	7	47	13240.	13210.	0.4500	-0.19
64	1	9	2	2	53	12960.	13180.	0.4542	-0.21
65	0	4	4	4	49	13310.	13260.	0.4708	-0.23
66	4	3	2	8	46	12980.	13130.	0.4625	-0.18
67	2	5	2	6	45	12900.	13150.	0.4625	-0.18
68	0	4	2	4	43	13050.	13070.	0.4708	-0.16
69	0	2	4	7	34	12520.	12610.	0.4875	-0.14
70	0	5	3	5	31	12710.	12740.	0.5000	-0.13
71	2	7	2	6	32	12590.	12720.	0.5000	-0.11
72	0	2	3	3	28	12580.	12650.	0.5125	-0.10
73	2	5	2	4	29	12570.	12610.	0.5208	-0.10
74	0	4	2	3	28	12270.	12390.	0.5208	-0.09
75	0	4	2	3	27	12170.	12250.	0.5292	-0.07

CYCLE NUMBR	NEGRO LEAVE	WHITE LEAVE	NEGRO ENTER	WHITE ENTER	TOTAL VACNT	AVERG COST	PRIC AVERG	PROP NEGRO	SEGRE INDEX
76	2	4	2	5	26	12280.	12400.	0.5292	-0.10
77	2	5	1	2	30	11860.	12250.	0.5250	-0.13
78	1	3	5	4	25	12020.	12010.	0.5417	-0.12
79	0	3	1	4	23	12250.	12130.	0.5458	-0.08
80	2	5	3	1	26	12440.	12200.	0.5500	-0.10
81	1	2	1	2	26	11940.	12150.	0.5500	-0.11
82	2	2	2	2	26	12000.	12130.	0.5500	-0.13
83	0	4	4	2	24	12030.	11960.	0.5667	-0.12
84	3	1	4	7	17	11860.	11710.	0.5708	-0.07
85	2	3	6	2	14	12030.	11950.	0.5875	-0.04
86	0	1	4	2	9	11830.	11780.	0.6042	-0.01
87	0	1	3	5	2	12010.	11970.	0.6167	0.02
88	2	4	3	1	4	12780.	12230.	0.6208	0.02
89	0	2	1	2	3	12350.	12350.	0.6250	0.02
90	1	1	3	2	0	12740.	12590.	0.6333	0.03
91	2	2	3	1	0	13370.	12930.	0.6375	0.04
92	2	1	2	0	1	13420.	13130.	0.6375	0.03
93	1	0	1	1	0	13470.	13320.	0.6375	0.03
94	2	2	3	1	0	13980.	13670.	0.6417	0.03
95	1	0	1	0	0	14350.	13750.	0.6417	0.03
96	1	1	2	0	0	14610.	14000.	0.6458	0.02
97	1	1	2	0	0	15050.	14300.	0.6500	0.01
98	3	2	4	1	0	15290.	14980.	0.6542	0.01
99	2	1	2	1	0	15440.	15270.	0.6542	0.00
100	2	0	2	0	0	16030.	15460.	0.6542	0.00

CYCLE NUMBR	NEGRO LEAVE	WHITE LEAVE	NEGRO ENTER	WHITE ENTER	TOTAL VACNT	AVERG COST	PRIC AVERG	PROP NEGRO	SEGRE INDEX
101	0	1	1	0	0	16620.	15620.	0.6583	0.00
102	2	1	2	0	1	16010.	15780.	0.6583	0.00
103	1	4	0	1	5	16180.	15860.	0.6542	-0.01
104	4	1	1	1	8	15820.	15920.	0.6417	-0.03
105	0	0	3	1	4	16160.	16070.	0.6542	0.00
106	0	4	2	2	4	16290.	16110.	0.6625	-0.03
107	1	2	1	3	3	15870.	16120.	0.6625	-0.02
108	0	2	3	2	0	16640.	16330.	0.6750	0.01
109	2	2	0	3	1	17420.	16850.	0.6667	-0.00
110	2	3	1	0	5	16850.	16900.	0.6625	-0.03
111	2	2	1	3	5	16990.	17170.	0.6583	-0.05
112	1	1	2	2	3	17460.	17270.	0.6625	-0.04
113	1	2	1	1	4	17340.	17340.	0.6625	-0.06
114	2	2	2	2	4	17260.	17360.	0.6625	-0.04
115	1	3	2	1	5	17800.	17450.	0.6667	-0.00
116	2	2	4	1	4	17900.	17810.	0.6750	0.01
117	0	2	1	0	5	17550.	17830.	0.6792	0.01
118	3	4	5	0	7	18170.	18050.	0.6875	0.00
119	2	0	0	1	8	18590.	18080.	0.6792	0.00
120	0	0	4	2	2	17970.	18050.	0.6958	0.03
121	0	2	2	1	1	18200.	18010.	0.7042	0.03
122	3	1	1	0	4	18820.	18030.	0.6958	0.01
123	0	0	2	2	0	18590.	18470.	0.7042	0.03
124	1	5	1	0	5	18470.	18530.	0.7042	0.01
125	1	0	0	1	5	18990.	18520.	0.7000	0.01

CYCLE NUMBR	NEGRO LEAVE	WHITE LEAVE	NEGRO ENTER	WHITE ENTER	TOTAL VACNT	AVERG COST	PRIC AVERG	PROP NEGRO	SEGRE INDEX
126	3	1	2	1	6	19290.	18790.	0.6958	-0.01
127	2	1	2	2	5	18310.	18670.	0.6958	-0.01
128	2	1	1	4	3	18860.	18820.	0.6917	0.00
129	1	5	0	1	8	18940.	18720.	0.6875	-0.06
130	1	0	0	1	8	18810.	18810.	0.6833	-0.07
131	0	0	1	2	5	18660.	18900.	0.6875	-0.04
132	2	2	1	3	5	18810.	18950.	0.6833	-0.05
133	0	1	1	4	1	18500.	18850.	0.6875	-0.00
134	1	2	3	2	1	19150.	18880.	0.6875	0.01
135	0	2	1	0	0	20000.	19290.	0.7000	0.02
136	3	1	2	1	2	20490.	19730.	0.6917	0.01
137	2	1	1	1	2	20180.	19960.	0.6917	0.01
138	1	1	1	1	2	19980.	20090.	0.6917	-0.00
139	2	0	2	2	2	20380.	20200.	0.6875	0.00
140	3	2	2	3	3	21070.	20540.	0.6833	0.01
141	3	1	0	2	2	20700.	20870.	0.6792	0.01
142	0	0	0	2	0	21410.	20850.	0.6792	0.02
143	3	1	2	2	2	21890.	21100.	0.6667	0.00
144	1	0	2	1	0	21290.	21320.	0.6708	0.02
145	1	1	0	0	0	22380.	21610.	0.6750	0.01
146	3	2	1	1	2	22690.	21770.	0.6708	0.00
147	3	1	2	3	2	22490.	22160.	0.6625	0.01
148	1	1	1	0	2	23110.	22560.	0.6667	0.01
149	1	3	0	0	5	22010.	22610.	0.6667	-0.01
150	1	0	0	0	6	0.	22610.	0.6625	-0.02